# IT'S A SIGN, STUPID!
# Navigation for the Spiritual Journey

Michael Ferdinand Joseph Doria

Copyright © 2013 Michael Ferdinand Joseph Doria

All rights reserved.

ISBN:1494810492
ISBN-13:978-1494810498

# DEDICATION

IN LOVING MEMORY OF MY MOTHER
Nancy A. Doria

DEDICATED TO
Elena Doria
Without you, this book would never have been written.
I owe you the Universe!

IN APPRECIATION OF
All middle children

SPECIAL THANKS
Shaliz & Robert Afshar
I'm forever grateful for your words of encouragement.
Much love and thanks for pointing me to the light!

SPECIAL THANKS
Adam Christ
We met in the fourth grade and we'll forever be in the fourth grade. Your humor, heart, inspiration and guidance are a rare find and cherished greatly.

# CONTENTS

**PROLOGUE**

**PART 1: NEAR DEATH EXPERIENCED**
Chapter 1: Mother's Day — Pg. 1
Chapter 2: Cape Ability — Pg. 10
Chapter 3: Breaking News — Pg. 17

**PART 2: NOTABLE**
Chapter 4: I'm with the Band — Pg. 29
Chapter 5: Tuning In — Pg. 34
Chapter 6: B.C. — Pg. 39

**PART 3: NIGHT OWL**
Chapter 7: Madison Avenue — Pg. 45
Chapter 8: Animal Instinct — Pg. 55
Chapter 9: Something Fishy Going On — Pg. 61

**PART 4: NOW YOU SEE ME**
Chapter 10: Happy Birthday — Pg. 68
Chapter 11: Manifesto! — Pg. 72
Chapter 12: Eye of Newt — Pg. 80

**PART 5: NEW GUY**
Chapter 13: Numbers Game — Pg. 88
Chapter 14: Fix-o, Change-o Rearrange-o — Pg. 96
Chapter 15: We All Fall Down — Pg. 101

**ACKNOWLEDGEMENTS** — Pg. 109

**ABOUT THE AUTHOR** — Pg. 111

# PROLOGUE

About ready to head home, on what was the eve of my last day in the world of news reporting, I got called into my boss' office. He began with the formalities that precede any awkward conversation and then got down to what I interpreted as "the last laugh". I wouldn't have my last day of news reporting. The day I'd just wrapped up was in fact my last. The station felt I was somewhat of a risk and feared I might say something stupid.

First of all, anyone who watched one bit of my news reporting in Las Vegas was only doing so in anticipation of what would come out of my mouth. In fact, it was SOP for the newscast. I never needed a script, rarely had a filter and still managed to be professional, respectful and informative. It was part of what made the morning news in Las Vegas a bit more bearable. And, not to toot my own horn but "beep, beep" - it was a big part of our jump from 4th to 1st place ratings in the morning. I knew just how close I could come to the line without crossing it, knew when to resist bringing out what I call my inner jackass and essentially knew better in general.

You might be thinking how naive I must be to assume that any station wouldn't make that kind of call. You're 100 percent correct. I was naive. Not the foolish naive, rather the optimistic naive. Optimistically naïve people hold on to an ideal the world is still filled with authentic, caring and mankind-minded human beings who only want success and the best for others. Regular naïve people are naive to their own naivety and the fact there is another type of naive. So After 11 years total on television -- having interviewed everyone from the homeless man on the street to our nation's first lady; and covering everything from a house fire to the September 11th attacks from ground zero; this was how I was going to sign off -- silenced. No on-air goodbye to the anchor I had most admired and appreciated out of all the others throughout my career. No farewell — wishing me the best in my endeavors from the team. Nothing!

I mean, really? Why would I publicly ruin my reputation by saying something vindictive toward the station on live TV? Who would be that stupid? And, what chance would I have of getting hired elsewhere after having pulled a stunt like that? Whatever intention I had of looking for another job in television news -- which was less than very little -- had all been lost. Plus, I loved Fox 5. I'm not afraid to admit I asked to stay despite the station's decision for my departure

As I walked out the door without any direction, job prospect or keepsake from my obnoxiously messy desk which I hadn't bothered to clean, I unknowingly stepped into one hell of an adventure that had no advanced warning. At least any advanced warning I could see. It is one that has you overflowing with every emotion imaginable. It brings you face to face with fears and forces you to put even simplicity into perspective. It has you silenced and awestruck at some points and screaming your face off at others. It back tracks you into your past then flings you into the future -- literally. It encourages you to open up, shut down and think before you speak. It attracts new friends and leads to goodbye with others you loved whole-heartedly. It reaffirms all you've ever believed and come to know in the world and asks you to vanish some of your existing viewpoints. It's not an adventure in which you ever ask to embark -- it is one you are called upon to do. You don't have the option to say no — usually — and you can't turn back once you begin. This adventure, this unique path, this insane but serendipitous quest is my **Spiritual Journey.**

And ca-ching! What a lucky son-of-a-bitch I was getting to do this in no other than Las Vegas, NV. Yup! The most famous win, lose or draw city in the world. Just the place you'd expect to figure out your place and purpose in the world. The obvious place to become better acquainted with God - or whatever his or her name is. Sin freakin' City! The place where you find everyone from the hopeful to the has-been and it might even be the same person in the same week. The city where some think the car pool lane is for one or more cars. The city where your best chance at a decent conversation on any given day is with the guy stuck working the Starbucks drive-thru. The City where some sincerely view ambition, goals or advancement as fancy living and others see it as a cowardly run away from your problems. <---- think about that. The city where there is no "I" in team, but there most certainly is an only "U" The city where you sarcastically tell a friend he might as well sleep at the bar (hoping he'll read between the lines), and he instead uses it as a bonafide solution. The city where only your birthday celebration would take place at a bar with a misspelled sign out front reading "The Crews Inn," instead of "The Cruise Inn." The city where people actually have to be reminded to not leave pets in the car with the windows closed on a 115 degree day. And, the city where despite all the above mentioned, you turn the tables on yourself announcing to the attendees at your going away party that you'll instead be staying put.

The truth is; I love Las Vegas -- a ton. This town has some of the most articulate, creative, risk-taking, mind-changing, loving and intriguing people you could ever meet. It's a sun up to sun down star studded town with a maverick m-o and applaudable attitude problem. It's home. I spent 11 years hop-scotching from city to city to chase a career I'd grown to detest. Moving again would be nothing more than a band-aid fix. Besides, who am I to determine where to start this spiritual journey? It began in Las Vegas for a reason. A reason I needed to discover. And guess what -- most of the ups and downs in my life, all the bullshit coated in layers of more crap, all the moans and groans -- were my own damn fault.

As you read this book, please do so with the following in mind. Spirituality and religion are not one in the same. In fact, I would encourage people who really want to get to know God to spend less time at church. Much like Buddhist principals, please accept or reject any of my insight. I would encourage you to search for answers and ask questions. I did my homework. I would ask that you keep an open mind and open heart. Enjoy the different perspective, writing style and structure you'll find in this book. Dig deeper into some of the concepts. Some of what I will discuss I have learned or adopted from others. They will get proper credit. The title and subtitle of this book are straight forward. If you look at something as just an ordinary, literal sign — then it's a sign. If you look at it with an open mind, it could very well be a *"sign."* The word stupid is not meant for you, unless of course you are stupid. Apply it accordingly. The word stupid is meant for me. The book truly is Navigation for the Spiritual Journey. You should know I am the textbook middle-child who was ignored growing up. I am a Pisces and a firm believer in the Zodiac. I have an overactive and finely-tuned intuition, the gift of empathy; partial psychic ability and a mouth that easily gets me in trouble ~~sometimes~~ **all the time.** I also whole-heartedly believe that words -- both written and spoken — have immense power and should be used carefully. Prayers are real.

Lastly, before you read further, I fully understand that in some cases this book chose you. It chose me. I'm the only writer in the world who had no ambition to write a book, yet here it is. Writing is a gift given to me through some greater force in the Universe. I was called to write it and will explain why later. If you think I'm feeding you a line of hocus-pocus mumbo-jumbo, then don't read the book. This isn't about money, fame or notoriety. I care about only a few things in life and to the highest degree possible. writing, music & art, freedom and mankind. In fact, I'll show you how as a young boy I wished my life into what it is without even knowing until

I was in my mid 30's. Now, let's begin -- and in all sincerity, thank you for giving me a chance to explain myself.

# PART 1
# NEAR DEATH EXPERIENCED

CHAPTER 1
# MOTHER'S DAY

The school bus had just come to a stop in front of my house. I was a fourth grader and finally home for the day. I remember the bus route used to make no sense because although I lived within five minutes walking distance to school, I had to ride the bus which went to the farthest stops first. I was — and still am — a very impatient person in life. I'm working on it but fear it may never change. What the hell? I'm not perfect.

As I was just about to get up from my seat on the bus, I looked up at our house. My mother was opening the window of the upstairs bedroom shared by me and my brother. I don't just mean the blinds. She opened the window **and** the screen. I thought to myself "What is she doing?" Then I got a warm sort of stinging feeling that I often did when I knew something wasn't right. I said to myself "I can't believe she's actually going to do it," then prepped myself for the impending embarrassment.

From that upstairs window, she flung four yellow bins filled with toys into the front yard. GI Joe went air borne, He-man and his sidekicks were hurled and whatever else was in those four bins was now part of the landscape in the front yard. All of those action figures got just that -- action! I didn't even bother to look at any of the other students as I made my way down that seemingly never-ending aisle to exit the bus. What was I supposed to say? "Want to come in for milk and cookies?" Before I even got the front door open -- and I'm not even kidding -- you could already hear her screaming at me and my brother. It, of course, included the familiar phrase in our household "wait until your father gets home."

SIDE NOTE: And parents wonder why their kids grow up the way they do!

In the week or so leading up to this apparent monumental moment in my life, my mother had been nagging my brother and I to clean our room and organize the bins. Yes, you read that correctly -- organize the bins. It wasn't enough that the toys would just be picked up off the floor and placed into the four yellow bins that fit nicely under our bunk beds. The bins had to be organized by toy type. I mean, really?

Multiply this situation by 400,000 and you pretty much get a painted mental picture of what it was like for me growing up. But as a former reporter, it would be very unfair to only give you one side of the story.

My mother always made sure that my brother, sister and I had everything we wanted for Christmas. Our birthdays were the same way. My mother made sure we were taken care of. But, she was the epitome — and then some — of strict when we were growing up. There, of course, was the middle child factor that also kicked in. That being my older sister of 5 1/2 years got the attention that comes with doing all the firsts as a child -- the prom, the driver's license, etc. My brother, Tony, is only 11 months younger than I. To put that another way, when he turned 14 years old we were both 14 years old for two weeks until I turned 15. This situation, when two siblings aren't even a year apart, is known as Irish twins. He was the football player, fisherman and troublemaker. In fact, I'm convinced that he was the sole creator of trouble. My parents' attention was focused on him a lot. There I was in the middle — Ignored. I will talk more at length later about being the middle child and how despite the cons that come with that territory, the giant plus side that exists and that I've come to discover in my spiritual journey.

Fast forward from the fourth grade to the year 2000. No sooner did the ball drop ringing in the new millennium, I was packed up and moving from my very first TV reporting job to my second. From Binghamton to Albany, NY. It was also quite the market jump too. The pay -- not so much. But, it was still better than making $17,000 a year and deciding between noodles and noodles for dinner nightly!  Another plus -- my cousins Chris & Angie and their kids Danielle and Paul lived in Albany. Paul was away at school. Danielle and I are the same age and both huge music lovers.  She's a beautiful singer and piano player.  Chris is my Godfather. And, Cousin Angie made one hell of a traditional Italian Sunday dinner.  Her pasta was perfect.  In my time in Albany, I think I only had to turn down one Sunday dinner invitation.  Live without a home cooked meal long enough and you jump at the chance when one is offered.

On a Sunday afternoon, just one month after starting my new job at Fox 23 News in Albany, I was about a half hour from finishing my weekend reporting shift. The phone at my desk rang.  It was my cousin Chris asking if I wanted to come over for dinner. I said absolutely but told him I just wanted to go home first and change my clothes and freshen up. When I arrived home, I could hear the phone ringing in my apartment. I quickly scrambled to get the door unlocked and picked it up. It was my cousin Chris on the other end. I told him I'd just gotten home and was going to change and head over to the house. "No," he said - "Angie and I are going to come over." This seemed a little strange — why would they come to my place after inviting me to dinner at theirs? Perplexed, I said ok and hung up the phone. That's when I got that warm stinging feeling in my stomach again. It was one of the stronger stings.  Something wasn't right. Something was up. I immediately called home. My Aunt El answered the home phone at my parent's house. "What's going on?," I said. This caught her off guard — she wasn't expecting my call. She didn't know at the time — nor did I — that I have a very strong intuition. She replied "Wait until your cousin gets to your place."   I already knew what happened. Trust me, you just know. "Don't fuck with me, Aunt El -- what's going on?" I will never forget this phone call or what came out of her mouth for as long as I live. "Your mom died," she said.

"Don't tell him that over the phone El," my father said in the background. To be completely honest, I don't really remember what happened next. I hung up the phone and went into shock. When my cousin Chris and Angie arrived at my door, I opened it with just a sickened look on my face. I was devastated. "I already know," I said. Then I burst into tears and started packing for what would be the longest, most depressing trek I'd make in a lifetime. For the next three hours I was in my cousin's car heading home to Rochester, NY.

You would think as a reporter I would've asked a few very important questions such as "what happened?" or how she died. But, just the mere thought of a dead parent is enough to stop anyone in his or her tracks. I was 24 years old — a few weeks away from turning 25. My mother and I are so much alike -- precisely the reason she and I would fight off and on as I was growing up. Living on my own is when I really started to enjoy talking with her. I was looking forward to the many more milestones in life I could share with my parents now that I was old enough to appreciate their company. I was also at an age where advice from parents didn't come with such confrontation. I appreciated it.

A little ways into the trip home, my cousin turn to me and asking something along the line of why there was a gun in the house. I turned to him and said, "What? What do you mean?" He said, "They didn't tell you?" "No, tell me what?," I said. My cousin got this look on face, hesitant to say anything. "Oh my God, I said, "She killed herself?"

The vision of my mother putting a gun to her head and pulling the trigger is very troubling. My mother certainly had her moments of depression. She was very neurotic. She was a lunatic of sorts when she got in one of her moods. But was she suicidal? I never once entertained the idea that she could or would go down that road. Looking back on it, it makes total sense. When you play Monday morning quarterback in a situation like this -- a lot becomes much clearer. And, when you're a lot like your mother, you become scared and concerned for your own life.

My mother's funeral was jam packed with people. Neighbors who had since moved that we hadn't seen in 10 or more years, old coworkers of hers -- the list goes on. Despite her moments, my mother had that magic touch with people. She was very well-liked. Much like me, she spoke her mind -- but she was respectful and respected.

For the next 10 years I tried to wrap my head around her death. Anger played a big role. In conversation, people would always ask whether she left a note. She didn't. Believe me, I checked. I learned that just prior to blowing her brains out (sorry -- it's just a thing that helps me cope) she was out in the garage cleaning the inside of her car. My mother would get pissed if a crumb only an ant could see were on the floor. It was aggravating. So; leave it to her to make sure we had a clean car to ride in on the way to her funeral. Without a note, there was much to the imagination about why. The answer, at least my answer, came while at a bar in Las Vegas one evening and knowingly on my spiritual journey.

My friend Mike and I were sitting on our usual side of the horseshoe shaped bar chatting. He had recently lost his father. I was there to induct him into the "Dead Parent Club." It's not a legitimate club, just one I created to laugh about this sort of situation. It's incredible how many of my friends -- all around my age -- are members of the club. It is rare that I meet a person these days that still have both parents. (**It's a Sign, Stupid!**) I believe that God puts them in my path for a reason. There is something therapeutic about sharing stories and making some sense out of this tragic situation.

As kids, we think our parents are invincible and will be around forever. As adults, we sometimes don't realize the short amount of time we have to enjoy their company.

Despite being at the bar to console Mike, somehow the conversation led back to my mother. I remember telling him that when I was a teenager in high school she told me that she had always wanted to be a News Reporter. Then, I remember saying something about how angry it made me that she could take her life and not think about all the other people that would affect. "I would never do that to someone else knowing how this feels," I said. What came out of my mouth next brought a look of shock to my own face followed by a flood of tears. It even stunned my friend Mike. It was a revelation that took 10 years to surface. One that could only come about while on a spiritual journey. "Maybe my mother had to die to save my life," I said to Mike. Let me explain.

The truth is, for as much as I am an over-achiever in life, I also used to give up really easily when the going got tough. I didn't believe in myself for a very long time. My mother's death was, in part, was the impetus to get my head thinking otherwise. I was also a very angry person in life — often pissed off at the world. Her death helped me change my mantra. I've had many achievements in my life that I had no idea were going to be in store for me. Many of them came through news reporting and many others after that career. I can say with certainty that if my mother hadn't committed suicide, I would probably not have pushed myself as hard as I have to get to where I am in life. I became the news reporter she aspired to be. Because of her choice regarding death, I can't and won't give up. Her choice with death is what gives me the daily drive to continue to try to be the best I can in life. Isn't that what all mother's want for their children — the best? I can honestly say my mother's dying saved my life. It really did. Period!

My discovery and understanding of why her death had to happen is not something that's going to sit well or make sense to some people, but hear me out. In life, God puts certain people in our path. People come, people go. Those people are in our lives for one reason or another and for whatever amount of time necessary. We are also in peoples' lives for a reason. Sometimes we are in someone's life for a very particular purpose. Think of the trickle-down effect. If my mother were alive, I may still be a news reporter. If I were still a news reporter, I might still be that angry person. Think of this scenario. A young boy starts to run out into the road. A stranger who sees the impending danger runs out to protect him and ends up getting hit and killed by the car. The boy grows up to be a doctor who ends up saving hundreds of lives through his practice. Had the boy not lived to fulfill his destiny, so many other lives would have been at stake.

Death doesn't always have to be the case -- it's just an example. Consider this scenario. I had a friend Nick for a short time in Las Vegas. He auditioned for the band I had formed. For the next couple months we became pretty tight. It was one of those rare friendships in life. We connected on so many levels. Our bond in music was just the icing on the cake. Nick, however, was not the happiest of people. And, he was addicted to pain pills. He ended up moving back home to Texas for treatment and a change of scenery. I was upset. Sure, I wanted him to go home, deal with his demons and get clean. But, it was still tough to watch him leave after we'd become such good friends. We kept in touch for a little while. Then, phone numbers changed and that was the end of our communication. About a year and a half later I received a text message at work. The number was unfamiliar. It was Nick. A few minutes later we were chatting on the phone. He was moving back to Las Vegas. I was ecstatic. Even better, he was clean. On the phone he said he always remembered what I told him before he moved back to Texas. I told him something I had learned from someone else. Imagine you have only one piece of dog food each day. When you wake up in the morning you have the choice to feed either feed the white dog or the black dog. Which dog are you going to feed? This scenario, which speaks about the importance of staying positive, was something I'd learned from Chris Howard - A Regional Vice President at a company called Primerica. I couldn't believe Nick remembered that. I was so thankful that little scenario was part of his successful recovery. Someone had passed it along to me. I in turn passed it along to him.

Nick moved back to Las Vegas a month after our phone call. We spoke via phone once. We never spoke again. How could this happen between two people who had become such good friends? My theory: Nick was in my life at just the right time and for the amount of time for which he needed. Maybe God and the Universe intervened and stopped us from reconnecting again. Maybe Nick is now helping someone else who needs a friend and some healing. I look at it this way. I'm thankful for the time I did get to spend with Nick. I'm even more thankful that he has recovered. Who knows, maybe Nick might not be around at all if it weren't for me. I've stopped questioning why people come and go.

Parting ways with someone or experiencing the death of a loved one can be detrimental or a situation from which to learn and grow. For me, focusing on the positive within the realm of the "reason" has been healing and a source of closure. My take on mother's death may be very different from what brother, sister & father all believe. That's absolutely okay. Whatever sense they make or have made of it is just as valid. The bond a mother has with each of her children is different and unique. That's the beauty of a mother.

My Mother's Famous Quotes:

"Do I look like I just fell off a Christmas tree?"

"I'm tired of cleaning up this house and watching you kids mess it up again. Do I look like an octopus on roller skates?" (Octopus would sometimes be swapped with Wonder Woman)

"We'll see what your father thinks when he gets home. Then you'll really be in for it."

"Make me come in there" (except she was already halfway down the hallway and actually coming into the bedroom to yell at me and my brother)

"Talk to me like that again and I'll slap you into next Tuesday"

**"I love you"**

## CHAPTER 2
# CAPE ABILITY

"HELP," I screamed -- then went under. I came back up, screamed again and just happened to notice a familiar face this time furiously swimming toward me in the water. I went under again. A few seconds later, someone grabbed me and pulled me safely back to shore. It was my older sister. All of this played out in less than a minute's time. I couldn't have been more than 8 or 9 years old. We were on a family vacation to Cape Cod for the week. It was the first of many times I would experience the beauty, power and control of the ocean. I had been walking on a sand bar in the water and stepped off of it by accident. I was far enough out to where the water was well over my head. I could have drowned that day had no one been around. This is the type of terrifying moment that you'd almost expect to scar a person for life. I could have forever been dissuaded from stepping into a lake, ocean or other overwhelming large body of water ever again. The backyard swimming pool might've forever become my worst enemy from that point on. But this was not written in the stars.

For starters, I'm a Pisces. I'm a water sign. Pisces is characterized by two fish swimming in the opposite direction. My big sister is a Scorpio and another of the three water signs in the Zodiac. Although I can remember that day and the terror vividly, I don't recall talking about that moment very much after it happened. The only scenario that did play out after that day was one of me forever embracing water thanks to my sister's "Cape Ability" (which I will explain in just a moment) and protective nature.

From the seventh grade through my senior year, I was on the school swim team. I even made Captain my last year.

I'm certain I spent more time in a Speedo during my high school days than I did in regular clothing. In addition to being on the swim team, I also taught swimming lessons to little kids on Wednesday and Friday nights, right after practice. On Friday nights, after practice and teaching swimming lessons, I was one of a few lifeguards on duty during public open swim. Becoming a certified lifeguard was not easy. The written test was tough. The water test was brutal. I was among the handful in my class who passed the first time. I have great respect for lifeguards.

Aside from that one moment in the ocean in Cape Cod, I have never been afraid of the water. Even large bodies of water don't scare me. In fact, I swam three quarters of the way across Keuka Lake on another family vacation seven years after the Cape Cod incident. I would have gone the distance but my mother would not allow it. She likely wouldn't have allowed me to attempt any of it out of fear I would drown. She was very overprotective at times. My only saving grace that day was that she and my father were out on our boat three quarters of the way across the lake. I swam out to where they were anchored and relaxing. I was almost 16 years old. Aside from that one day in Cape Cod, I've always felt safe in the water — connected.

Now, back to my point -- and my sister. She displayed what I refer to as "Cape Ability" while in Cape Cod. (Note the instances of the word Cape - **It's a sign, Stupid!**) Cape Ability is my way of describing the awesome, super-hero like ability that takes over people. It refers to that flood of adrenaline that allows someone to swim like mad out to the person who needs saving. It's the superhero strength that forces someone to run into a flame-filled building when the lives of others are at risk. No doubt, you've all heard the stories of people lifting cars off of others who are pinned underneath. When you encounter a person who displays this type of "Cape Ability;" pay attention to him or her. These are people who genuinely care about the well-being of others. They are a blessing. They believe in the good that exists in the world. They believe in mankind. They don't even have to contemplate or rationalize helping someone else. They just do it. On a whole other level, they are the people who truly want the best for others. They are nurturers and protectors. It's in their nature.

My sister recently told me that to this day - she is still terrified of deep water. You would think otherwise; right? But her heroism that day is exactly what protected and saved me from having a fear of water. Being around water is my source of creativity, comfort and peace. It's part of my zodiac sign. It's part of my DNA almost. Had water been a fear in life versus a source of inspiration, I would not be the person I am today. My life would have turned out much differently. It's incredible to think how one tiny moment in time could've had such enormous effects had circumstances been different. My older sister saved my life both literally and metaphorically.

There is another incredible type of "Cape Ability" that people possess. These people have such power and influence on the world. Their abilities send a vibration globally.

Over the course of three Olympic Games -- Athens (2004), Beijing (2008) and London (2012) -- we witnessed greatness on top of greatness compounded by more greatness from one particular man. Just walking away a gold medal winner one time is ultimate glory in my opinion. Leaving an Olympic Games dubbed as "unprecedented" is colossally monumental. I don't even know what words are appropriate, or whether any even exist, to properly portray the historical moment created by Michael Fred Phelps. I point out his middle name because my first middle name is Ferdinand, or Fred, when translated to English. Phelps was born on June 30th which makes Cancer his Zodiac sign. Cancer, like Scorpio & Pisces, is a water sign. You haven't forgotten that I'm a Pisces and former swimmer and that my lifesaving sister, Gina, is a Scorpio, have you?  Now, to learn Michael Phelps is a Cancer and fellow water sign seems a little interesting huh?  **It's a Sign, Stupid!**

The eight gold medal wins in Beijing, on top of the other 10 gold medals won during his Olympic tenure — plus the 2 Silver and 2 Bronze he acquired — left him with a grand total of 22.  With that medal count, he is the most decorated Olympian of all time.  The kind of blood, sweat and tears that went into the making of this story is off the charts. Anything I could write about it would be a gross understatement. But, think about the outcome apart from the fame and notoriety Michael Phelps gained.  There's the new and even higher level of inspiration and motivation he created for other athletes.  There's the attention and respect he called to the sport of swimming -- a sport that never had enough of either.  There's the influence he had on kids; especially those enrolled in swim clubs and programs.  There is even the possibility his acts of greatness become just the inspiration needed for other swimmers to go on to be Olympians.  You see what I'm getting at.  The vibe he sent through the universe was massive.  And, this doesn't even take into account the money-making and commercial opportunity sides of the coin that were born out of Phelps' participation in the games.  The vibe he created -- THAT is also Cape Ability. The idea that one man could wield that kind of power and create such a ripple effect is incredible.  His hard work and immense dedication paid off and went viral in the sense of how many other people were touched in a positive way.  We don't get to meet these people often.  If you do get the chance, point out their greatness and thank them for making the world a better place.  I did!

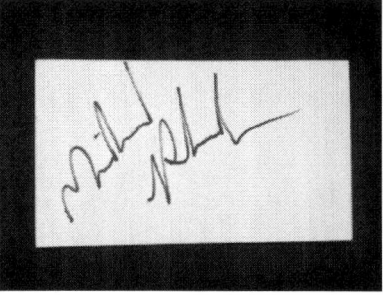

While covering a red carpet event for my freelance reporting gig one day, I spotted Phelps making his way down. I knew he was going to be at this particular event I was assigned to cover and was thrilled at the chance to meet him. Typically, at red carpet events, publicists will come down the line asking each reporter if they'd like to speak to a particular celebrity. The publicist will then do his or her best to make it happen. In this instance, I was told he wasn't talking to press. Naturally, I was disappointed. However, I also learned from my news reporter days that if you take no for an answer — you'd have a justifiably short journalism career. I apply this concept to many situations in life. No means "not now." It doesn't mean no.

Notice how much taller Michael is than me in the picture. His height was a perfect opportunity, I thought, to allow me to get his attention. I shouted his name and jokingly flailed my arms to point out my shortness. "Down here," I said. It worked! When he looked over at me, I pointed to myself and said, "Former swimmer -- I'd love to shake your hand." Now, who is going to say no to the person who wants to shake your hand? And, I sincerely did - he's just an amazing man. Not only did I shake hands with Michael Phelps and thank him for bringing some much needed publicity to a sport I hold near and dear; I then got him to answer a couple of questions needed for my assignment. I then convinced him to take a picture with me afterward and even got his autograph. How did I manage to get so much after initially being told that he wouldn't be speaking with the press?

Simple; I put myself in his shoes. Phelps wouldn't come out of the pool with just one gold medal. He would come out with many. He's a warrior. He's focused. He has the right attitude in life. I left that red carpet with four gold medals that day. I had my story, my photo with Michael, his autograph and the handshake. The things you accomplish by stepping into the shoes of an Olympian!

As a child, I was just as obsessed by Greek mythology as I was with superheroes. Each God or Goddess having his or her own domain or power over a particular area was fascinating. It still is! I read a headline somewhere during the Olympic Games that questioned whether the Olympians were actually Greek Gods. While at first pass the question is seemingly rhetorical, I chose to interpret it a different way. Maybe Michael Phelps was pulling energy from Poseidon - the God of the sea. And, if he were, so could we. In fact, we could pull energy from any of the Greek Gods to help us in any area of life.

Consider and test my following example. If you're looking for love, why not tap into the Goddess of Love herself; Aphrodite? Her Roman counterpart is Venus. Aphrodite is portrayed as having a beaming smile. She views the dove and sparrow as sacred animals. If you do a bit of further research on the spiritual meaning and symbolism of animals, you learn the dove is symbolic of hope, new beginnings and maternal instinct. The spirit of the sparrow symbolizes joy, friendliness. When you blend the spirit of Aphrodite with the symbolic meanings of the dove and sparrow, doesn't this make an interesting combination? Ladies — doesn't this make a list of the best ingredients for a perfect love potion? Gentlemen — doesn't that combination make the most incredible scent of a woman? It's safe to say a person is much more attractive when beaming with joy and friendliness and shining a beautiful smile.

The theory works just the same if you're a man looking for love. Instead of Aphrodite, use the Greek God of love -- Eros (Cupid in Roman Mythology). Research his associated animals and their spiritual and symbolic meanings. Harness the power and spirit of Greek deities and animals! I've included charts below to get you started. You might one day be saying, "Oh my God or Goddess."

| LOVE | GOD/GODDESS | ANIMAL SPRITS | YOU |
|---|---|---|---|
| Women | Aphrodite (Venus) | Dove, Sparrow | |
| Men | Eros (Cupid) | Dolphin | |

***Love Chart:*** *For the "You" column, write in your best attribute or quality and let it also shine from you while harnessing the power of the God/Goddess and the animal spirits.*

| KNOWLEDGE | GOD/GODDESS | ANIMAL SPRITS | YOU |
|---|---|---|---|
| Women | Athena (Minerva) | | |
| Men | Hermes (Mercury) | | |

***Knowledge Chart:*** *Want to gain more knowledge? Well, that won't happen if I do all the work, stupid! Do some research, fill in the boxes and come to a conclusion. After all, knowledge IS power!*

I pointed out the importance of paying attention to people who possess the various kinds of Cape Ability. Just as much as they are heroic in some ways, they are also teachers. They get us to think about and tap into our own abilities. We're all capable.
But, wouldn't it be great to be Cape Able too? Now, let your inner super hero soaring!

## CHAPTER 3
## BREAKING NEWS

The countdown had begun in my ear. "5..4..3.." Timing is everything when it comes to TV news. Throw off the timing behind the scenes and it becomes very noticeable to the viewer. The earpiece a reporter wears is crucial. "2..1..mic up & cue," said the producer in my ear. My live shot (as it's termed in TV news) was from Saratoga Springs just outside of Albany, NY that evening. I put together a story regarding the many benches removed from the sidewalks in the business district. Too many kids had been loitering in front of businesses. The ticked-off owners were tired of losing business from would-be patrons put-off by the crowds of kids.

By all accounts it was a very easy story. Textbook journalism. Storytelling 101. "Good evening Ann & Greg," I said to the anchors — while taking a quick peek at the small television monitor positioned a few feet in front of me. That monitor shows the reporter exactly what the viewer is seeing at home. To have one on a live shot was also somewhat of a luxury due to equipment always being faulty or kaput. "The good news: not all benches were removed so you can still find a few," I said as I continued with my on-air introduction before the minute or so long taped insert package would play. The insert package is the part of the story on tape with the reporter's voice over track mixed with interviews. It's just a tighter way of providing further detail on a story. "The bad news: areas like right here -- where there are no more benches -- no place to **shit**. Uh, **SIT**! Excuse me!"

Now, thank God I had that insert story running or I would've been stuck, on live TV, turning 20 shades of red through all the make-up I was wearing. How the hell could I have just said "shit" instead of sit? Even worse, now I was one of "those" reporters in the market. No one would ever take me seriously again. This, of course, if I even still had a job after that kind of slip-up. The "S" word was taboo -- one of the forbidden four letter words on TV during certain times. With the thought running through my head that the station could get fined if the FCC happened to be monitoring that day, I quickly called the producer. "Tiffany, I can't believe I just said that -- is Dave (the News Director and my boss) mortified?" "Mortified?" she said. "No - we are all pissing our pants in the control room. That was hilarious."

This very same faux pas would manage to once again come out of mouth later that year. It was intentional. I was taping a spoof story to play at our annual company Christmas party. It seems my slip up was one for the history books too among employees because no one ever let me forget that live shot.
I was a bit surprised by how easy it was to brush off that slip of the tongue and even poke fun at it. For a very long time during my career as a reporter I was intense out in the field. I'm the epitome of a perfectionist. I can count on one hand the number of times another reporter from different station had beaten me while on the same story. I talk about why later in the book.

During my sophomore year of High School, I'd made up mind with regard to my career path. I would become a News Reporter. Through "A graded" papers from my English teacher, I had discovered I was decent writer. Plus, my parents did always say I'd make a perfect reporter considering my nose was always in everyone else's business. It's 100 percent true. It was to the point where my parents would frequently replace my name with that of well-known gossip columnist Rona Barrett when they'd catch me snooping or eavesdropping. If for some reason I weren't able to cut it as a reporter, I'd settle on becoming a lawyer. This was another career for which I seemingly had encouragement from my parents. To the defense of my brother or sister I came whenever they were in trouble. I would argue why they should be exonerated. I, of course, knew the truth first-hand. I'd been snooping. I was also the king of always needing to have the last word. These skills earned me the nickname F. Lee Bailey after the famed and accomplished defense attorney. Nosey and argumentative — this was a killer combination for anyone looking to make a mark on the 6pm news.

During my college commencement ceremony, while sitting under the hot sun and working on what would be a fantastic burn on my forehead in the shape of the graduation cap, my mind was racing. I had just one day off in between graduation and my first "real" job. On that following Monday, I would make the daily trek into downtown Rochester, NY to serve as the morning Production Assistant on News 10 NBC. I recall someone saying this was the fastest they'd seen someone find a job after college - and that always stuck with me. My undergrad work was four years of filling up my schedule with whatever would get me ahead in life. Starting out in the print Journalism track, I eventually switched to Broadcasting. In my last year of college I had the hardest schedule to date. My senior year was comprised of a full course load both semesters, a senior honors TV project where I had to produce, shoot and report five in-depth stories off-campus, two part-time jobs (one at the dining hall, the other as McDonald's manager), two internships (1180 WHAM news radio and 13 WHAM-TV) and Vice President of my fraternity, Pi Kappa Phi -- a position that heavily focused on recruitment and retention. Looking back, I have no idea how I managed all of this. But, I had a goal. I was determined. I was going to be a news reporter and nothing was going to get in my way. At the age of 22 I left Brockport State College with a Bachelor of Science degree in Broadcast Journalism and with a feeling I'd never previously experienced. For the first time in my life, I was proud of myself -- wholeheartedly proud of myself.

Just six months into my production assistant job at the NBC affiliate, I said goodbye to the station and to the only city I'd lived to that point. I packed my car and journeyed 2 1/2 hours to the Southern Tier. My apartment, positioned above a bar in Johnson City (Binghamton), had no kitchen, no bathroom of my own, no running water, and needless to say, no charm. Here I was with a college degree paying $200 a month to live in squalor and poverty. My annual salary as a reporter at News Channel 34 was $16,000. I made more as a McDonald's Manager. You could only imagine my delight when I was eventually promoted to weekend anchor and handed a fat raise. Now living large on $17,000 a year, I was also bumped up in socioeconomic status to middle-class dirt poor. (**It's a sign, Stupid!**).

I left Binghamton and my first reporting gig after a year and three months on the job. The enticement of a lead dayside reporting position at the Fox station in Albany, NY was too good to pass up. Plus, it came with a $25,000 annual salary. I also left Binghamton with a friendship that would become a major influence in my life -- a friendship put into place by the hands of some greater force in the universe. This is the kind of friendship with which you are humbled and honored. Sitting diagonally across from me in our pod of desks in the newsroom from day one in Binghamton was Kristen Miranda. A fellow Italian and morning news anchor at the time. She was a different kind of girl. She didn't need to wear a lot of make-up. She didn't have to raise her voice. She didn't have to tell you something twice and she didn't have to demand any attention. She was the right amount of all the good qualities in a person. People were drawn to her. Her aura was magnetically inviting. (**It's a Sign, Stupid**) When you meet someone like this, pay very close attention. A big part of a spiritual journey is taking a closer look at and understanding all the people with whom you've come into contact throughout life. With both the short-lived friendships and those for the long-haul, you will learn that hidden inside a few of these people are answers to some very important questions you've been asking yourself for quite some time. I call this the "Answer Period." As much as it is an enlightenment and learning phase, it is also a reality check of sorts. You may need to reconnect with some people with whom you've had a falling out. You may need to have the "Come to Jesus" talk with others. And, be prepared, as you may need to part ways with others. Like love and war; all is fair in this process. The ultimate goal is finding the real "you" and understanding your mission in life. On the journey, you'll know the right times to retrace your path and examine some of these friendships. My Aunt El, for whom this book is dedicated, taught me to use the "if, then" hypothesis approach to find answers and come to conclusions in my journey. It's brilliant and it works!

The millennium hit and Kristen and I were quite tipsy at one of those New Year's Eve parties you remember forever. The next day, I said goodbye. I tearfully left Binghamton and journeyed 2 1/2 hours North to Albany, NY. Settling into this city was difficult. With the passing of my mother, there was little joy or solace in anything that came my way for the next year. Couple the sadness and mourning with anger and I'm sure I appeared as a glowing beacon of light to everyone. I decided to bury myself in work and focus on my career. Albany was an interesting city. We didn't cover politics much despite being the Capitol of New York. I found myself covering a lot of death. Enter the September 11th terror attacks.

There are certain stories a reporter will always remember in television news. During the course of my coverage of the 9-11 attacks, the "Cell Phone Lady" grabbed my heart tightly. I think about her to this day. To better explain, this is the blog post I wrote on 9-11-13.

*"One story I'll never forget. 12 years ago today -- at this very hour -- I was headed from Albany to NYC to cover the September 11th attacks. In fact, at this point we didn't know*

*if they were confirmed attacks. I'm not sure if it was luck or a curse that my photographer and I managed to find the one side street that hadn't been blocked off. We both said "Let's go for it." 45 minutes later we were standing at ground zero. My eyes couldn't have been bigger; my jaw couldn't have been dropped wider. People covered in dust, debris everywhere and disbelief just as widespread. A total sense of defeat. The next three days were some of the most awful I'd had as reporter. Sure, I had the story -- but that was the problem...I had the story. As I was interviewing a woman on my final day in NYC, she distinctly said that her missing husband -- who was among the many buried in the rubble -- was probably just waiting to use his cell phone and saving the battery for when he needed it. That, according to her, was the reason she couldn't get through to him. I almost started crying. In fact, I did...just not while on the story. This was also the first time in my career I'd been speechless. I was 24 years old. In a city of millions and millions of people, this poor woman felt alone and abandoned. The man she loved, the man with whom she made a lifelong commitment and the soul mate whose side she swore to stand by forever was gone -- for good. After she uttered those words "he's probably just waiting to use it," that was my cue to stop the interview. She knew he wasn't coming home. But, she was not about to let me or anyone else steal any more from her. That tiny piece of hope and long shot that he was alive was all she had left. I always wondered -- and still do to this day -- how she handled the next few days, weeks and months. I've interviewed first ladies and vice-presidents -- My reports have shut down ill-run businesses and I even got a railroad company to spend hundreds of thousands of dollars in replacing faulty tracks and equipment at crossings. But the one story I remember the most is the "Cell Phone Lady" from 9-11. Do me a favor. Give your significant other, your brother, sister, mother, father --whomever -- a kiss and hug today. The only story I really got -- and the only one worth remembering while covering the September 11th attacks — was one of true love and the senseless separation of a couple. Remember the victims today, but also remember that we as humans are built to love. It's not something to be taken for granted."*

After two years in Albany, a reporter position opened up at the ABC affiliate in my hometown of Rochester, NY. This was the station where I had done my internship in college. It was the number one station in the market. I interviewed and got the job! From Albany to Rochester, I headed across New York State where I would spend the next five and a half years of my reporting career. When I stepped back into the newsroom I'd once graced as an intern, everything was the same as when I'd left. All except one thing. Sitting diagonally across from me in our pod of desks in the newsroom was Kristen Miranda. (**It's a Sign, Stupid!**)

What's interesting about the spiritual journey is it's one that starts long before you ever knowingly embark. There are situations, people, places, etc. that are put in front of you months; even years prior. Once you "sign on" to the journey, it creates a unique opportunity to really understand why certain people, for example, are in your path. Kristen and I are still friends to this day. We chat at least once a week, usually via text or social media. In my journey, I've come to learn that there are certain qualities of hers that I need to possess or take on. To put it another way; the journey is, in part, about watching certain people — especially those with whom you have a real connection. That connection is strong because it's the Universe trying to tell us something. Sometimes, other people possess particular qualities that will help you in life if you pick up on the signs and adopt some of those qualities. Kristen and I crossing paths again was not coincidence. In fact, I don't believe in coincidence at all in this world. Everything that comes our way — as freaky or weird as it may seem — is for a reason. We may say or think it's coincidence. But it isn't.

**EXERCISE:**
Think of a friend with whom you have a particularly strong bond. Try to figure out what qualities he or she possesses that may suit you well too. Now, borrow a piece of jewelry from that friend for a week. Make sure it's expensive so you can pawn it. I'M KIDDING! As you approach certain situations and circumstances in that week, use the piece of jewelry as a reminder to get you to imagine how that friend would act or react. Only elicit the positive or admirable qualities of that friend. I think you'll find this will help you and your relationship with this friend. After all, the wiser man is one who can see things from multiple perspectives.

Rochester was a news market that brought another of those stories a reporter will never forget. This was a story that also chipped away at my soul and ultimately led me to make an exit from TV news. His name was Andrew Attinasi. He was my age — 26 years old. He thought he'd be a gentleman one summer night and walk two girls home from a bar down on East Avenue. He didn't want them walking alone. Rochester had a terrible gun problem and even bigger murder rate in the city at the time. But, not necessarily in the part of town where Andrew had been walking. Encountered by a thug, Andrew was told to "drop his pockets" (empty his pockets) by the count of three. Andrew reached in. 3-2-BANG! He dropped dead in front of the two girls he was walking home. In his pockets -- nothing of significance or value. Despite his compliance with the thug's orders, his life was taken. Another senseless death!

The next day I was face to face with 15 or so of his friends in the backyard of Andrew's parents' house. It took every ounce of energy to keep from bursting into tears that day. I had covered death a zillion times. This time, it was too close to home. It was one of those moments that smack you across the face. Rule number one in journalism — keep your emotion out of the story. I couldn't. Watching Andrew's friends sob while I was interviewing — I too started crying. His death was unfair. He was being nothing more than a gentleman that night. He did not deserve to die. But, God had a plan and a purpose. Still, I was angry.

**To Andrew's friends and family: My heart goes out to you. Although I never met Andrew, I do know that he was a wonderful person with a heart of gold. I will never forget his story - ever!**

By September 2006, my heart had practically hardened. As I've said, cover enough death and that will happen to a person. By this point in my life, you could put me smack dab in the middle of a funeral and I wouldn't flinch. All I cared about was getting the story and getting the hell out of there. That's not right.

I had no idea what working in my hometown would bring. I just knew that if I were going to keep any sense of sanity, I had to get out. I was becoming bitter. The only career I'd ever seen myself in was becoming a prison. I hated getting up for work. The creativity I'd once known as a kid was somewhere deep, deep inside — nowhere close to the surface. I made a promise to myself. At 30 years old I would move across the country. Job or no job. I needed a new coast, a new perspective — a new everything. I was five months away from turning 31. Time was running out. It was now or never.

It just so happened the News Director at the NBC affiliate in Rochester (the station where I began my first job out of college) had moved to Las Vegas to be the chief of the Fox affiliate. It also just so happened; a reporter position had opened up. In two weeks time, I had an interview and a new contract as the morning reporter at Fox 5 Vegas. I bought a one way ticket to Sin City where I would spend at least the next three years of my life on-air as the morning reporter.

Las Vegas was unlike any market I'd ever worked. You could get away with murder (no pun intended) on the morning news. In fact, I was dubbed "The Loosest Cannon" in TV news for the things that came out of my mouth. I called a guy a douche-bag on live TV, took my shirt off while covering President Obama's visit, danced to any number of pop songs quite frequently, used the light stand in our station gear as a stripper pole, made fun of the male anchor's haircut non-stop and made some of the most wonderful friends a person could ask for in his career. (**It's a Sign, Stupid!**) It was the most fun I'd ever had in TV. This was the side of me that people deserved to see. It was the side of me that came naturally. I wasn't the bitter, angry guy I had thought. Yes, I always delivered the news factually and with integrity — but also with fun and flair. Our morning team was dynamite. We all brought unique personality to the table and blended well with one another. You'll meet another member of the team later in the next chapter of the book. Our overall team chemistry seemed like a hit. Not too long after I started, we were greeted by the ratings that essentially grade us on our performance. Judgment Day was here.

The once fourth place ratings on the Fox5 morning news quickly shot up to first place. We were number 1! The anchors, producers and my fellow reporters on the morning show — we were all ecstatic. We rode this train for all it was worth. It was exciting. I couldn't go anywhere without someone saying hello, asking for my autograph or telling me how much I made them laugh in the morning. In 2008, the newspaper of record in Las Vegas, The Review Journal, awarded me with "The Best Reason to Wake Up in the Morning." It's the only award I'd ever received in my news career. It's the only one I ever needed. (**It's a Sign, Stupid**) My destiny, as you'll learn in a later chapter, is to be an "Uplifter" in life. It's quite an amazing feeling when you're fulfilling your destiny.

As they say in life, all good things must come to an end. Being passed up for weekend anchor (now for a second time in my career) was just part of the equation that led to my exodus from TV news. Also, after three years, the station decided not to renew my contract. It happens. It's quite common, in fact. I don't fault the station one bit for making that decision. It was the best move for both parties. After 11 years in TV news — I was spent. I had come to realize the career I'd once revered in life was one I'd started to loathe. Now, I had an even bigger decision to make. Do I stay or do I go? Do I leave what I'd worked all my life to attain? Or, do I pack up and move on to another city and join another news team? I was becoming someone I never wanted. Jaded, pessimistic and even angrier. Ask any reporter and all will tell you that stories take their toll emotionally and leave a long-lasting imprint. I didn't want to go through life feeling nothing. I didn't want to have no reaction when people died. I didn't want to remain straight faced when someone got exciting news. I wanted to be human. If I stayed in TV news, I would eventually die, metaphorically. Instead, I left the business altogether when my contract expired. The good news: I left **near death experienced**, not dead.

# PART 2
# **NOTABLE**

CHAPTER 4
# I'M WITH THEBAND

When a new song comes out that perks my ears, the entire world knows about it. It's on auto-repeat; I sing it everywhere and ultimately wear it out. I'm a music maniac. But equally as important to the notes, chords and catchy hook in a song are the lyrics. After all, I'm a writer. My favorite musician is — and always will be — Alanis Morissette. Whenever she comes out with a new album, I'm both excited and perplexed. If I didn't know any better, I'd swear she were a peeping Tom watching my every move and jotting down findings. It's odd how every one of her records is so relatable to my life and at the perfect time. (**It's a Sign, Stupid**) When an artist speaks to you in this way, pay very close attention. It's God trying to speak to you — connect with you. Hear me out.

Especially on the spiritual journey, you come to realize that God is all around us. God is that tree in your backyard. God is your pet dog. God is the couch you sit on in your living room. Think about it. If God created people and a person made that couch (or part of it), then isn't God part of that couch? Isn't God in that couch? Reach in between the cushions and shake his hand. Also, quietly put any change you find in into your pocket — it adds up. I digress. So, if God is in all of us, that song Alanis Morissette wrote is an extension of God. Now, you might be wondering how many artists fit in with this theory given their lyrics and content. That's easy. If a particular artist has the power to save a life, help someone out of a dark place or move a person to move mountains all by way of a song — that's God. As complex or simple; if it has the power to speak to a person — how can we deny the song that works this kind of magic?

One morning, while sitting in the live truck awaiting my turn up on the news, my photographer and I were chatting. He too is a music lover and was in a band at the time. When I blurted out "I think I want to be in a band," he quickly replied "You can't be in a band." And with those words, I went into warrior mode. Don't ever tell me "I can't." I've had my fair share of people in life tell me what I could and couldn't do. "That sounds like a challenge," I said to him. (**It's a Sign, Stupid!**)

About a month later, I was the lead singer of "90 Proof" — a band I created. It was a 90's alternative cover band and for the next two and half years we played all over Las Vegas. We even got paid to do so. (**It's a Sign, Stupid**) You never forget the first time you see your name in lights or on a flyer. The rush on stage is incredible. What I didn't realize at the time — I was conditioning myself to gain more confidence in life. I could get in front of TV camera and speak with ease. The audience was invisible. Yes, people were at home watching, but they weren't all literally huddled up in front of me watching as I delivered the news. When you have a live audience sitting in front of you — and you're singing — the nerves come out. It took me a good year to get comfortable singing in front of people. Sure, I did it at karaoke all the time. But, when you're in a band — the crowd comes to see you only. Not 20 or 30 other singers in an evening. When you're on the spiritual journey, you learn that circumstances and situations that are put in place for a very particular reason. In this instance, it was two-fold.

On the one hand, it's a very humbling and rewarding experience to be in a situation that is uncomfortable. This is how we get stronger in life. I view it as "resistance training" for the soul. When we find ourselves in situations that are awkward, scary or even deemed impossible by our own regard, we tend to run. We tend to chicken out. We tend to "resist" and find excuses. This could be true with anything in life. Think about the resistance that comes when a kid must move and start attending a new school. Think about the new duty at work we didn't ask take on. Think about the new diet we keep pushing off. Think about that big speech we must deliver but don't want to give. We spend so much time "resisting," we often don't look ahead to the bigger picture or to what sits on the other side. I've come to learn that nine out of 10 times, there is some beauty on the other end of whatever it is we're resisting. There's a lesson. There's a situation — whether in the immediate or distant future — for which we are being prepared. Some people stick it out and learn to resist the resistance. Others fight it beyond belief.

I'll be the first to admit it's not easy to resist the resisting. We're trained at a very young age to resist. We also live in a very "immediate" society. With social media, smart phones and the internet, we have everything at our fingertips. We want it "now" because we've been conditioned to expect it now. To have to wait for anything is torture. Incidentally, you should see me sitting impatiently in traffic. I'm sure I look like a lunatic to other drivers. I want to get where I'm going quickly! I resist the calm commute I could be having. As another example, I would suspect people who start going to the gym stop soon thereafter when results aren't noticeable instantaneously. They're impatient. They're resisting.

With resistance training, the end result isn't always immediate. As mentioned, we're sometimes being prepared for something ahead. If truth be told, I believe some of the reasons for the band and opportunity has yet to be presented. I have an idea as to one of the reasons which I'll share with you in a later chapter titled "Manifesto!."

There were some great rewards that did come with being in a band that I have already enjoyed. Sitting in the audience — at nearly every show — was Shirlise Castille. (**It's a Sign, Stupid!**) She, like me, is a music maniac. We met at another musician's show. It wasn't until I started seeing her at mine that we really connected. She believes in me as I do in her. We've been to numerous concerts together and she is trying to break into the music business. We talk quite frequently and she reminds me of the importance of never giving up in life. She's a Godsend. Who knows? Maybe one day we'll both be in the music industry and helping one another out. There's a reason she was always sitting in the audience — beyond just the friendship between us that formed.

I can also unequivocally tell you that a challenge is a challenge is a challenge! We have to challenge ourselves sometimes. We need others to call us out in challenge. It's the nature of the human being. How do we get good at what we do if we don't challenge ourselves? The band challenged me to prove that I could get up on stage with my fellow band mates and put on a show. It wasn't something that I would spend my life wondering about had I not done it. The challenge of being in a band was also the impetus to accept other challenges in life. What's great about the challenge is the end result is sometimes an unknown or something completely unexpected. We may find the initial challenge was really just a minor player to get the ball rolling. Think of it this way. A mother is selected to organize a baked goods sale at her kid's school. She's frantic. She's never done this before. She doesn't even know how to bake. In the course of organizing, she's learning as she goes. In the process, she decides she should bake something to contribute to the sale. Low and behold, she's just baked the best pie anyone has ever tasted. A hidden talent came out! This mother decides, after a couple years of continued baking, to open up her own bakery. Business booms and she's a success. You see how the organizing of a simple baked sale led to an end result she was not at all expecting? Need I say more?

Okay, well I'll say just a few more things. The most important ingredient this aforementioned woman had was courage. Accepting the challenge is always the hardest part. Having the courage to do so is noble. It separates the men from the boys and the women from the girls. Accept challenges in life. What's the worst that could happen, success? And, should you not succeed does not mean you've failed. You never fail in life until you give up. Got it? Good!

What I also learned from being in the band is that while I do enjoy being on stage singing — it's not really what I want to do. I discovered that I liked writing songs much better than singing and performing. Had I not gotten on stage, I might never have discovered that. As a band, we performed cover songs. But, as an individual, I had started trying my hand at songwriting. To be a songwriter, you must be able to sing the songs — in front of people. The band forced me to really think about all the instruments and their importance. My ears were more finely tuned in the end. The band was merely the conduit to perhaps an eventual career in songwriting. Who knows?

One last thought on the reason I created a band in the first place. Remember those challenging words from my news photographer telling me "I couldn't?" Maybe that was God getting through to me in the way he knew I'd listen. Had the photographer told me I could start a band, I probably wouldn't have done it. The photographer telling me otherwise was enough to get me fired up and going. Don't always assume someone is just trying to aggravate you by the words they choose. Maybe God is trying to get you to listen and take action.

CHAPTER 5
# TUNING IN

I remember the day like it was yesterday. I was 12 years old and driving in the car with my mother. I'm sure it was cold outside because Rochester, NY only has two seasons: Winter and Construction. My mother would often sing in the car, but very faintly. She had a decent voice, but would never sing very loudly. A popular song at the time called "The Living Years" by Mike & The Mechanics came on the radio. My mother immediately grabbed hold of the knob on the stereo and turned it up. "Listen to this and pay attention to the lyrics," she said. I sat quietly in the car and listened to the song. After the song finished, she lowered the volume and asked if I understood what it meant. I replied "yes," but she explained it anyway. (**It's a Sign, Stupid!**)

To paraphrase, the song — in a nutshell — is about letting go of gripes and grievances we may have with our parents. We may not always agree with them or see things from their perspective, but life is too short to let those barriers get in the way. What I particularly like about the song is that it encourages us to actually have open dialogue with our parents to talk about the tough stuff. At least in doing so, there's a chance to come to an understanding and reconciliation.

What confused me at the time was my mother's insistence on my listening to the song. I didn't know her father, my grandfather, very well. The reason being - he was ill and had suffered a stroke. He was in his 80's when he passed away. Growing up, we would make a trek to the VA Hospital each weekend to visit him. On Thanksgiving and Christmas, we would pick him up and bring him to the house to spend with family. But my grandfather's stroke affected his speech and overall cognizance. He was impossible to understand. It was heartbreaking to watch at times. I remember being afraid or uncomfortable when I'd walk into his hospital room. It was not an easy process. "Hi Grandpa Joe," I would say with no real response back. He was looking at me, but there was no connection it seemed. This was tough for a young child to understand.

The only one who could truly understand him was my mother. She adored him. Years after he passed away, while I was in my sophomore year of college, I was taking a woman's studies class. Our big project was to interview a woman who was significant to us. I chose my mother. What I had learned is that my Grandparents were extremely strict with my mother and her sister (my aunt) while they were growing up. If my mother got out of line, she would be punished. I imagine she was told "No" a lot because she was not so easily swayed or convinced when my brother and I wanted to do practically anything. Getting a "yes" out of her took an act of God. When she was teetering between a yes and a no, she deferred to my father for a final ruling. "What did you mother say?" was his usual response. As you could imagine, my brother and I had to have a lot of strategic meetings to determine a game plan and the best parent to approach initially for permission granting purposes. It was a headache.

I remember one summer; it took weeks of convincing to get her to let us sleep outside in the backyard tree house with some friends overnight. "So help you God if you leave the yard while you're out there," she said. And, of course, we left the yard. And, of course, we were caught. It was all my brother's fault - naturally. I was an angel. Our punishment: grounded the entire summer. We couldn't leave the front yard and no friends were allowed over to play. I'm not even kidding. About mid-way through the grounding I just assumed my mother would let up and allow us freedom again. Nope! When she said the entire summer, she meant the entire summer. Even when pointing out the friends who were also grounded for leaving our yard that night had served their sentence and could roam freely, she didn't care. From that point on, my brother and I learned to reserve our summer troublemaking for the month of August. School started in September and provided a nice change of scenery from being grounded to the confines of the front yard.

Whenever I'd hear "The Living Years," a song I grew quite fond of, I would always think back to that car ride with my mother. I wouldn't hear the song very often. In some cases years would pass before it would resurface. After my mother passed away, my father and I got closer than we'd ever been in the past. My brother was more aligned with my father while growing up. I was more aligned with my mother. My sister is a blend of both parents, as I see it.

In September of 2013, I marked my seventh year in Las Vegas. I was also having one of those months where looking at me the wrong way would possibly result in death rays shooting from my eyes. Yes, even on a spiritual journey, you have bad days, weeks or even a month. But, on the spiritual journey you tend to be more conscious of the bad days. They don't pass without some dissection to figure out why they occurred and the lesson to be learned. I was driving on the highway (and we all know how much I hate traffic) when my father called. Hands free, of course, I answered and we got to talking. It was one of those conversations where you find yourself getting more and more aggravated as it continues. In my seven years in Vegas, only my brother had come to visit. I'd only seen my father three times in those seven years — all of which were in Rochester, NY upon returning home for various functions. Once again, I'm the middle-child. Ignored. When I told my father that I had been contemplating moving to LA to break into screenwriting, his exact words were "Yuck, LA?" I got pissed. "I can't believe he can't just be supportive and happy that I want to try my hand at screenwriting," I said to myself. I had already proven that I was successful, responsible. Why the "Yuck?" He eventually passed the phone over to my step-mother so I could say hello but it was too late. I was in warrior mode. All I remember saying is "I'm annoyed and aggravated at you two and I'm hanging up." And I did. For the next five minutes, I'm sure I looked like a lunatic to other drivers watching me yell out loud with no one else in the car. For the next two weeks, my father and I didn't chat. He knew I was mad. Generally, he lets me cool off knowing that trying to talk to me to soon won't get either of us anywhere.

A week or so later, I was asked to be part of a panel for a TV show that a friend was putting together. The other person on the panel was a man named Frankie Scinta. If the name sounds familiar, it is the same Frankie Scinta who hails from Buffalo, NY and who has a show called "The Scinta's" in Las Vegas. If you come from any family, you will appreciate this show. If you come from an Italian family, you will feel like you're sitting at the dining room table at your house. It's genius. It's a musical show with a lot of impersonations, comedy and "play" fighting between two brothers. I hadn't met Frankie Scinta until we showed up for the panel. I hadn't even seen his show. As I was walking across the parking lot into the studio where the show was being taped, a man with curly black hair almost ran me over. Then he started laughing. As I walked up to the car window — all set to rip him a new one — I realized it was Frankie. I laughed. It *was* funny. Plus, he's a "paisano" and just has a likable aura. You can't be mad at this guy even if you tried.

When the taping was done, we exchanged numbers. He told me to give him a call when I wanted to come see his show. That next weekend, I asked him to see if I could get three tickets. I had two friends in town and thought this would be perfect. Plus, the show hadn't received one bad review. As we took our seats in the theater — right in the front row — Frankie acknowledged me and my friends. He then had the entire theater laughing at his antics for the next hour and a half. At the very end, as Frankie was thanking everyone for coming, the band started playing the first few notes of the last song in the show. I was paralyzed in my seat with my jaw dropped. Then my eyes welled up with tears. It was "The Living Years," by Mike & The Mechanics. My mother sure knows how to knock some sense into me even in the afterlife. The next day I called my Dad. We had a nice long talk and cleared the air.

And, if you still think this all might just add up to coincidence — here's further proof otherwise. My father, who is now retired, was mechanic for more than 30 years. My mother was suggesting that I — "Mike" — need to be the mechanic in this situation and fix the issues with my father.

## CHAPTER 6
## B.C.

I began writing my second album, an EP titled "B.C.," shortly before I was knowingly on what would be my life's spiritual journey. I found it very peculiar — yet comforting — that the mention or round about reference to God and spirituality seemed to be the undertone throughout this collection of songs. (**It's a Sign, Stupid**) Unlike the first album, "Neon Graveyard," which included a synthesized sound in every song; "B.C." was all written with the bass line in mind first and had a much more acoustic feel. (**It's a Sign, Stupid**)

Essentially, "Neon Graveyard" is the company for anyone's misery. What a dark, dark album. Don't get me wrong, I stand by every one of those songs I wrote. Some might even say it's not as negative sounding as I make it out to be. After all, songs like "I," "October Sweat," and "Impeccable Kiss," hardly resemble pessimism and purloined hope. But, the power and emotion behind those songs still come from a very angry time in my life. I truly believe that whatever you feel inside — whatever is going on inside you — that is what you are shining out to the world. People can see it and you can't hide or disguise it. So, despite the message in a song, I believe that people can still sense whatever emotion was present at the time it was written or recorded. This is also the reason, nowadays, I'm very careful with the timing of my writing. As a general rule of thumb, I try not to write when having a miserable day. Unless, of course, I'm writing something that requires that kind of energy behind it. The last thing I want is the wrong vibe being sent out into the Universe. Words have power! I'll say that again. **WORDS HAVE POWER!** I find it important to very cognizant of and careful with anything said or written. Words must come from the proper place within and be backed with the intended emotion. We have so much power to screw so much up due to verbal or written misplacement or displacement.

I generally only write with working titles in mind — be it a song, a chapter, a book — whatever! I'm not entirely sure why I do this. It's just one of those quirky, perhaps superstitious rules every writer adopts somewhere along the line. So, when I started my second album, "B.C." was the title that popped into my head. (**It's a Sign, Stupid**) What few people know is that "B.C." stands for Balance and Compassion. Little did I know, I was writing what would become two of the most simple, yet important words I'd ever write. Balance and Compassion or "B.C." wasn't just an album title. It was the title to my spiritual journey. Now, had I titled the album "C.B.," it would've been in the correct order. I got the compassion part down very quickly. The balance part was and still is the much tougher bull to ride. I'll talk about that in just a bit. When I realized later in my spiritual journey that I wished or prescribed the whole thing — with God at the helm of it all — this was mind blowing. How on Earth could I have written my own destiny or near future path without even knowing it? The truth is — as I've come to learn — we do it every day. Some of us are conscious enough to realize it while others let it slip by without the slightest raise of an eyebrow. I liken this album to Boot Camp when someone joins the military. It's a rigorous and grueling course meant to condition us for what's ahead. It's meant to get us into a habit — a routine. It's preparation. Here's the track list for "B.C.":

1.) State of Mind
2.) Punch Line
3.) Alter Ego (Acoustic)
4.) Half Awake
5.) Moonshine
6.) Freelancer

As another general rule of thumb; one adopted from the mindset of Alanis Morissette; I don't give away the meanings behind my songs.  Some are pretty obvious.  Others require some deeper thought.  The way I see it — I certainly wouldn't want to take away whatever someone derived from a song of mine with my explanation of what it really means.  Especially -- if it empowered or helped that person.  If I reveal the true meaning, the song may have less value to the person.  He or she wouldn't listen to it in the same way again.  Make sense?

But because I'm in a good mood, I'll give the readers of this book the exclusive inside scoop on State of Mind.  I wrote this song after learning about the concept of rewiring or retraining our brains to think positively — first, instead of the negative.  I learned this concept from my childhood friend Adam Christ.  He and I met in the fourth grade and we still talk quite often.  Oddly enough, he started his spiritual journey a few years before I did.  (**It's a Sign, Stupid**)  I guess I just didn't give his journey much weight or overall thought until I had started on my own.  Turns out, he wasn't the whack job I'd thought.  Just kidding Adam!  In his brilliance, Adam explained we tend to always go to the negative first — having learned to do so at a very young age.  When we didn't get our way as kids, we'd throw a temper tantrum.  As we got older and started dating, for example, a break-up was the end of the world — not a new beginning.  That extra work our bosses slap on us at the last minute is uncalled for or unfair.  It's not, instead, looked at as a test and needed learning for that big promotion.  Bottom line; we see the downside or negative angle in most situations first.  We don't tend embrace the light and joy they often hold.  So, if I may dissect the lyrics.  I won't go through the whole song, just parts.

## STATE OF MIND:

**The day started before it even began - lost in pretend.**

**I said it before and I'll say it again — don't know how, why or when.**

The first two lines of the song suggest that we are so routine with our negative mindset. The day is already lost if we can't figure out a way to shift our thinking to the positive. Jumping ahead to the first chorus:

**There we stood — separated — about to break, we couldn't see all the light.**
**Over there — overrated — a hint of truth, hidden in a clever disguise.**

The chorus reaffirms this routine that will keep driving us crazy if we don't break it. The light is the positive side of things we often don't look at first. Overrated refers to the negative side that many people consciously and unconsciously choose. It gets too much attention - it's overrated. But, because it's the prevailing side, it is unfortunately truth of sorts.

I also wrote this song from two viewpoints. On the one hand, this song was written for my friend Nick who I mentioned back in Chapter one. It was a way to guide him into this way of thinking — a path he was already on. On the other hand, the song is about the two side of me — the negative and the positive. After the first chorus, I up-tempo the song a bit and give it an electric guitar and more defined drum beat. The song switches from the negative to the positive. Here are the first two lines of the second verse.

**The night seemed to go on for like a million years — it had no end in sight.**
**Pushing buttons politely while collecting blank stares — but somehow it felt so right.**

These two lines come from the feeling you get when you don't want the night or a situation to end. It's so good and joyful you want it to last forever. You're pushing all the right buttons and people look at you oddly because your joy is beaming. They want to experience that same feeling. Truth is, anyone can experience this situation indefinitely should they choose to stay focused on the positive — not the negative. Moving ahead to the second chorus, I add another line.

**There we stood — separated — about to break, we couldn't see all the light.**
**Over there — overrated — a hint of truth, hidden in a clever disguise.**
**State of Mind — state of being — a brilliant seat reserved for the wise.**
**Train of thought — enforced and bleeding — taking back what's rightfully yours and mine.**

The first part of the chorus serves as the reminder to not relapse into the negative. The second parts offers up the idea that whatever state of mind we're in becomes our state of being. The train of thought must be enforced and almost bleeding life. When we think positively, we are taking back what is rightfully ours — we're in the right state of mind.

In 2008, when much of this album was being written, I had the opportunity to go to Europe. My roommate at the time was getting his Master's degree and studying abroad for a semester. Unsure of the next time I'd return to Europe, we decided to spend a few days in Italy before heading to Spain. Rome was only a two hour flight across the Mediterranean Sea. Three days there, followed by a week in Barcelona, was one of the most magical, eye-opening and inspiring trips to date. (**It's a Sign, Stupid!**) I filled up an entire black notebook of lyrics, rhymes, poems and thoughts during this trip. I also had a little inspiration from Alanis Morissette. Just prior to the trip, she released a new album, "Flavors of Entanglement."

Upon returning home from Europe, my mind was bubbling with song ideas. One morning, while in the news van, I had an epiphanic moment. While waiting for my turn up on the news, I wrote what I consider to be one of my most powerful pieces of work. I wrote "Half Awake." I should say, rather, that God (through me) wrote "Half Awake." It took 20 minutes to write from start to finish. The music didn't take long either. It was a song that popped into my head. I had no warning it was coming. This wasn't just a song. It was a prayer. My prayer! Think of it like the butterfly forming then breaking from the cocoon. It was my right of passage of sorts. In a way - now that I further think about it - it was God telling me "Out with the old, in with the new. You've been given a second chance, use it wisely and don't ever go back." It was my road to follow. It was my mantra. Here are the lyrics I wrote for "Half Awake," a song the world will hear someday — somehow.

FIRST VERSE:
**Five senses beware // You've but moments, to prepare**
**The things that I've learned // Can now be put into words**
**That man in the mirror // will vanish and a new one appear**
**I've cut off my tongue // and put new air in these lungs**

PRE-CHORUS:
**This road I will follow, will bloom different flowers**
**I've cleaned out my gutters, made room for God's water**

CHORUS:
**Goodbyes I've said**
**My gut is at peace**
**I've bid my farewell to being wide asleep**
**I've opened my wounds**
**Extended handshake**
**And my purpose is clearer now that I'm Half Awake**

SECOND VERSE:
**Fearful no more // I've shown my ego the door**

I won't raise my voice // new habit, but mostly by choice
My armor's torn off // my heart from solid to soft
I'm walking straight lines // to let moments come in due time

PRE-CHORUS:
This road I will follow, will bloom different flowers
I've cleaned out my gutters, made room for God's water

CHORUS:
Goodbyes I've said
My gut is at peace
I've bid my farewell to being wide asleep
I've opened my wounds
Extended handshake
And my purpose is clearer now that I'm Half Awake

BRIDGE:
I won't back down, I won't turn around, I'll stand my ground because

FINAL CHORUS:
I've said my goodbyes
My gut is at peace
I've bid my farewell to being wide asleep
I've opened my wounds
Extended handshake
And my purpose is clearer now that I'm Half Awake
Now that I'm Half Awake. Now that I'm Half Awake.

By the middle of 2009, "B.C." was done. I made it a point to sing each song on the album publicly somewhere. The music was done electronically. I spent hours manipulating and rearranging unlicensed snippets of digital chords and riffs. I will eventually enlist the help of musicians and real instruments make the album in the form I originally intend —

all acoustic. I'm currently learning to play piano. More on that -- in another chapter.

With all this writing, my level of compassion for all things grew tremendously. I had started to look at the world differently. I started to understand peoples' pain. I started to smile at their joys. For all intents and purposes, I was evolving into a human being again. When the journey began — or at least when I fully recognized its beginning — my heart would bleed over everything. It was beautiful. Even more, I couldn't believe I could write the manuscript for my spiritual journey. Once again, God reaching out to me in the way he knew I would listen.

What was noticeably missing from my spiritual journey was the "Balance" from B.C. Pisces are known as the chameleon of sorts. We have a unique ability to adapt quickly to situations and sympathize with both sides of the equation. We also sometimes ultimately become our surroundings. For almost two years after my departure from news, I was constantly studying, learning and working. In part, it had to be this way. I left my career as a broadcaster for PR & Marketing. This required a lot of training and learning hours. Quite often, I was in my room on the computer or with my nose in a book while friends were out at dinners, parties or shows. It was a tough two years, but it paid-off professionally. It didn't bode so well spiritually with regard to the balance I'd been longing for. The balance that was supposed to be a *notable* part of my journey!

# PART 3
# **NIGHT OWL**

## CHAPTER 7
# MADISON AVENUE

I'm not much of a TV watcher. Back in the day I had my list of shows to which I'd regularly tune-in but as I got slightly older I preoccupied my time with other things. One show I did regularly watch was "The Girls Next Door." It was essentially life at the Playboy mansion following Hugh Hefner and three blond bombshells. Holly Madison was among the cast members. There was something different about Holly. While she was a great choice for that part in the show, she was also smart and well-spoken. I picked up on this right away. As weeks and episodes went by, I started wondering why I was so drawn to this show. But, I sort of put it in my back pocket and carried on.

When I became a freelancer for a national celebrity magazine, I was on red carpets left and right interviewing celebrities. I never anticipated this happening and didn't even see it coming. I'm not one to get star struck. However, if I do ever get the chance to meet Alanis Morissette; rest assured you will hear the loudest, high-pitched shriek reminiscent of a 13 year old girl.

My experience with celebrities is much different. I usually find a question that perks their ears. I like really getting to know a person. I find out what makes him or her tick, what inspires him or her, etc. I do get told from time to time that I ask good questions. Maybe it's a gift — and not just the gift of gab. When Holly and I started crossing paths, I was excited to finally meet her. When we did, she was much different than on TV. She was very guarded, very cautious. I figured maybe it was just a moment. But it kept happening. She wasn't at all rude. She just wasn't as happy as I pegged her to be. (**It's a Sign, Stupid**) In many ways, she was a lot like me. One person on TV and another off. She is a very hard working performer. She was perhaps all work, though.

There was one particular time I was covering a mall appearance by a particular celebrity and Holly was one of the pool of guests in with the appearance. She was looking in a mirror fixing her make-up. I thought to myself "I feel like something's bothering her." Then I also thought, "Why are you so concerned?" The truth is in a spiritual journey, you're drawn to certain people for a particular reason — whether it's to learn something about yourself or to take on a quality of that person that you need. As time went on; and I started interviewing Holly more and more, something clicked. This once guarded girl had warmed up to me. In a way, it made sense. She'd seen me enough times. But, I like to think that she felt comfortable around me. I never wrote a bad thing about her. There's nothing bad to write. When she became pregnant with Rainbow, her daughter, she had the glow you'd expect to see in a woman. She was all smiles all the time. I could barely get the words out of my mouth and she was already beaming and pontificating about the joys of being pregnant. She was happy. During this time, I learned that, like me, Holly was also very artistically creative. She was painting a Disney themed mural on the wall in the nursery she was preparing for Rainbow. Fast forward a year or so and the engaged Holly Madison was now married. The smiles from her grew even wider. She was so calm, so at peace. And, now becoming the opposite of what I was in life — on edge and always running around buried in work.

During the summer of 2013, I created and produced a 15 episode podcast. As I do with everything in my life — I made it a big deal. Quite honestly, I don't know why I make everything such an ordeal. But, as a friend once told me — if you can't promote or believe in yourself, who else is going to do it for you? Ain't that the damn truth! For the first episode of the podcast, I wanted some star power. Holly was the first person I thought of. I created a segment called "Who, What, When, Where, Guy." I would ask female celebrities questions about men with hope that men would understand their ladies better. For example: Who is the man you most admire? What is the most romantic part of the evening when on a date? When is the absolute wrong time for a guy to try and make love? The "Guy" part of it was the one thing that woman just come to expect of a guy and one thing they're never going to change. After all, I gotta give some props to the guys. When I reached out to Holly's publicist to ask if she would do it, I got a very quick response back. "Yes, of course." I was elated. That's just the kind of heart you'll find inside of Holly. She's appreciative of all she has in life and will go out of her way to help someone else.

One day, while covering a movie premiere, Holly made her way down the carpet. She looked terrific as always. She gave me a hug and we said hello. But there was something that I'd never asked her before and was dying to know. "Holly," I said "You have such a different aura about you — you're glowing, you're happy — what changed?" I'll never forget her one word answer. "Balance," she said. (**It's a Sign, Stupid**)

I must have looked at her like she had 14 heads. In my mind the wheels were turning as if suddenly the world made perfect sense. In a sense, it did. The one thing missing from my journey was the balance I couldn't seem to find. The entire transformation I watched Holly undergo was God's way of showing me what I needed to do.

As I previously mentioned in an earlier chapter, I had worked so hard in college so I could get to where I wanted to be in life. The problem is, I never shut it off. I just kept plugging away. I even wrote off all possibility of finding love or having a family because I assumed my purpose was my job — whether it be a news reporter, marketing manager, etc. I never stopped to enjoy anything I had accomplished. When you don't stop to enjoy — or take time to smell the roses as they say — you're never content. When you're not content, you keep pushing forward hoping to find a sense of worth and completion. It's funny because for the last 10 years or so, I kept saying that something was always missing. I would have a great job but no significant other. Or, I had a significant other and great home life, but wasn't happy professionally. Somehow, the balance was always off or tipped too heavily to one side.

I've come to learn that you have to stop and take a breather every so often. If; for nothing more, than to appreciate and be thankful for what you have. I've also learned that there is nothing wrong with asking for more in life. Balance can also mean not having enough of what we need. If you need more of something, ask for it. If it's meant to be, your request will be answered. However, that doesn't mean you can sit on the couch eating popcorn and watching soap operas all day. You have to meet God halfway with requests. You have to make an effort. He's got your back. You just have to greet him with a handshake and a promise to do your part. It's probably a good idea to always make good on that promise too.

Imagine yourself as a bird gliding through the air with your wings spread. As a bird, you have your wings spread apart equally to allow air to hold you up underneath and keep you flying straight. When one of those wings drops, the bird turns left or right depending on which wing is lowered. That is balance in life. If that bird were to keep one wing lowered, it would spiral downward until it landed on the ground. The exact same happens when our balance is thrown off. We spiral downward. We might have the best of intentions with whatever it is that's throwing off the balance, but it doesn't always work. There must be some give and take.

When our balance is thrown off, we miss out on a lot of potential opportunity in life. We miss out on crossing paths with people who might help us or be beneficial to us due to our balance being shifted. We miss out on the potential for making new friends or even finding a lover or partner. We may ignore our child's recital or decline that invitation to a party because we're buried in other obligation. What if one of the guests at that party had the key or solution to your balance problem? When our balance is shifted too much to one side, our emotions also tend to follow. How many times have you seen the person who is all work and no play very irritable or too high strung? No one wants to be around this person. He or she is sending out an awkward vibe through the Universe. Should this person keep this up long enough, he or she soon won't have many friends. Relationships suffer. This person's health may also be jeopardized. The lack of balance brings about stress. We neglect our well-being when balance is shifted because our energy is too focused in one particular area. When balance is thrown off, we also tend to become sloppy in life. We apply band-aid fixes to problems, ignore other problems altogether or throw our arms up in the air and give up with other issues that come our way.

Finding balance is not easy. In this day and age, the level of responsibility and what's expected of a person has become quite burdensome. But, that's no excuse to ignore balance and the beauty life has to offer. There are seven days in a week. Each day brings about some opportunity for us to ground ourselves and reconnect with the Universe. Here's a starter chart to help you manage your life a little better. Use my suggestions for each day of the week or create your own.

Either way, try to carve out some time each day to stay sane.

| MONDAY | Sounds Like Mundane \| Get Ducks in Row |
|---|---|
| TUESDAY | Two for Tuesday \| Double Your Pleasure |
| WEDNESDAY | Remember When? \| Start Your Projects |
| THURSDAY | Sounds Like Thirsty \| Wine to Unwind |
| FRIDAY | Brain Fried? \| Let it Wander |
| SATURDAY | Renamed Siturday \| Sit & Read |
| SUNDAY | Get Some Sun \| Get Outdoors |

**MONDAY:** Get all the mundane done. Pay some bills, balance your checkbook, throw a load of laundry in the washer, etc. Balance is also making sure we stay on top of our responsibilities. If you can afford it — hire an assistant!

**TUESDAY:** Double your pleasure! Maybe you like to bake, draw, play piano, do crossword puzzles, etc. Whatever it is — spend twice as long doing this on Tuesday. When we double our pleasure we have just the right amount. We won't be too overloaded by it. And, we won't be missing it if we haven't had enough. It's two for Tuesday.

**WEDNESDAY:** Remember when you said I wanted to do that or get a particular project done? Do it. Today is your day to remember when. It'll put you more at ease by starting the project even if you can't complete it right away. It'll still be there next Wednesday.

**THURSDAY:** Sounds like "Thirsty." Pour yourself a glass of wine and relax. Don't drink? Blend up a smoothie and soothe yourself.

**FRIDAY:** The day our brains our fried. No sweat. Let you mind wander to wherever it takes you. Even if it's just for a half hour, it may be the much needed medicine to regain clarity and control over your life.

**SATURDAY:** Let this be the day you "sat" for an hour to enjoy a book, magazine, newspaper or even a rerun of your favorite TV show. Spend an hour calm and relaxed and you'll be thanking yourself later. Life isn't always about being in the fast lane.

**SUNDAY:** Enjoy some sunshine. Step outside and enjoy a quick bike ride today. Or snap some photos on your smart phone and enjoy nature. Bring yourself into the present. If you live in a snowy climate, bundle up and brave the cold. It's only for a ½ hour.

Balance, I find, is a lifestyle. Finding balance requires some trial and error. It also requires us to listen to others or watch them closely. Perhaps, through them, the Universe is trying to tell us or show us what we need to do. Who knew the road to balance in my life included a turn onto Madison Avenue?

## **EXERCISE:**
Draw a circle on a piece of paper. At the top, bottom, left and right of the circle put four areas of your life which occupy the most time. For some people it may be their job, family, charity, etc. Now, between each of those categories, put four sub categories that are also important but don't get enough time. When you spend a little time in each of the eight categories, the circle is flowing as it should. When one or two categories don't get the proper attention, or too much attention for that matter; that's when the circle breaks. Life is full of circles. But, as I see it, we should only be concerned with how the bigger circle is connecting.

CHAPTER 8
## ANIMAL INSTINCT

One afternoon, while outside at work to get some fresh air, a crow landed a few feet from where I was standing. "Eww," I said. The crow is one ugly, nasty looking bird. But, its apparent purpose that day wasn't for me to offer up all the negative attributes it possessed. I went back into work and thought nothing more of it. The next day, I was again outside for fresh air and to think as I normally did every now and again at work. Again, a black crow landed a few feet from where I was standing. "Crap," I said. "This is obviously a sign." (**It's a Sign, Stupid**)

When you're fully aware that you're on the spiritual journey, you don't tend to look at things the same way you once did. Signs become more apparent. You're subconscious awakens. You're more connected and in tune with what is going on in nature. You're closer to God. I went back into work and got on the internet. What I uncovered was another interesting puzzle piece of this journey. Animal Totems!

Like humans, animals have spirits. The spirit of the animal has some symbolic meaning. While I believe that any animal has this power or ability to give you guidance and insight, there are some that are more well-known for doing so than others. The crow is an interesting bird. It carries both positive and negative symbolic meaning. On the journey, I've come to learn that it's your job to figure out what it's trying to tell you. You must decipher whether its message is positive or negative with regard to what it's trying to get you to notice. While the crow can be a sign of luck, it can also be a trickster. Whatever the initial feeling you get when you see the animal, I believe, likely directly correlates with the message you're supposed to receive. For example, if you smile when you see the crow, this may be indicative of good luck. If you snarl, as I did, when you see the crow; watch out!

About the same time I saw this crow, I was looking for a new place to live in Las Vegas. I didn't have much time to find a place either — due to procrastination. I absolutely hate moving. It's such a process and a craps shoot at times when it comes to roommates. I eventually found a place on the South side of town and within the range I was willing to pay. The master bedroom of a house was open. A couple lived there but I'd have the upstairs all to myself. I went over to look at the house. All seemed ok. As the gentlemen who would be my roommate and I were outside talking, he said a couple of things that made me go "Hmm." I also got that warm stinging feeling in my stomach — my intuition was kicking in. "Fuck," I said.

Intuition is tough at times. When you have it — as Pisces do — it works overtime. It's a wonderful gift, but one that also leaves you second guessing because it works too well. I decided to ignore it. I shook the gentleman's hand and told him I'd be moving in. A day before I was to move in, something was still nagging at me about settling into that house. This is God's way of slapping some sense into me. Even if I ignore a sign, it's not for long. God will nag at me until I come to my senses. I thought about it some more and it finally dawned on me. Without further hesitation, I decided not to move into the house that sat in a quaint neighborhood on **Little Crow Avenue** in Las Vegas!

The good news is, I wasn't without a place to live for very long. I had friends - a couple — who I'd known for 10 years and needed a roommate. I didn't get a warm, stinging intuitive feeling so I assumed the coast was clear to move in. After I unloaded the moving truck, I sat down on the front steps for a minute to relax. As I sat there I heard a weird noise. I looked to my right and there was a hummingbird fluttering in front of one the flowers in the front yard. It was very close to me. "Here we go again," I said. Another sign! Ready for what the hummingbird means?

- Enjoyment, Lightness
- A Sign to Bring Playfulness into one's Life
- Denouncing Negativity
- Quick Response & Swiftness
- Independence
- Coming into the Present

The minute I looked at the hummingbird, I **smiled**. In fact, I laughed out loud a little and shook my head. God really does know best!

A couple weeks later, I had been recruited to be the PR & Marketing Manager for a firearms company. Naturally, this brought a lot vacillation. On the one hand, it was a great opportunity. On the other, it was certainly unfamiliar territory with regard to the product being sold. I accepted the position, but was still a bit uncertain. I was a week away from starting the new position. My new roommates had an extra pair of tickets to see Guns & Roses in concert. I took one and gave the other to a friend to join us.

While waiting for the concert to begin, I was standing (we had standing room floor seats) in the concert hall known as The Joint at Hard Rock Hotel & Casino. I overheard a few girls talking behind me. They were from Rochester, NY - my hometown. I quickly turned around to introduce myself and we got to talking. As the conversation winded down, two girls came walking up. They were chatting with one another and were from New York City. That's one accent you can't deny. As they moved in closer, one of the girls looked at me, pointed to my stomach and said "You're having issues, aren't you?" Without missing a beat, I replied "Yes, you must be a psychic." In fact, she was and she was dead on. I'd been having stomach cramps off and on for about a week. "Nothing to worry about," she said. Figuring I'd use the opportunity to get some more clarity and guidance, I asked her about the Octopus which I had been seeing lately and the dolphin which I had a dream about just a couple nights prior. "People are leaching off of you and using you," she said with regard to the Octopus. This is exactly how I felt at the time! As for the Dolphin, "The angel of the sea," she said. She further explained it was brought into my path to send me a message. To myself I thought, "But what was the message?" I knew the psychic wouldn't be able to answer that. I had to figure that out for myself. Also — I was coming into another realization that I'll talk about in a chapter ahead.

As the psychic and I finished our conversation, she turn around and was now standing in front of me. On her back shoulder was a tattoo of a dolphin. "Oh my God," I said quietly. At this very point, the lights went down and Guns & Roses came on stage. There was a screen that was part of the band's stage decoration flashing different images. About a minute into the show, I look at the screen to find images of dolphins swimming. "Holy Shit," I said to myself. I had a ring of people from New York around me — like dolphins do to protect someone. Then, it hit me like a ton of bricks. An answer! Guidance from God. "Go to the guns to get your roses," I said.

How powerful is that? I was nearly floored when the Universe gave me this message. So, what were the roses? Well, there are parts of the spiritual journey that are personal. And, while I've have some of them, I haven't quite received the full dozen I'm expecting just yet.

A bit more about animal totems -- there are also insect totems. Yes, even the preponderance of insects in our daily paths can bring about some clarity and meaning. However, make sure the circumstance is unique before looking into animal or insect totems. For example, I wouldn't necessarily expect a big revelation while you're at the local zoo. You went to the animals, they didn't come to you.  Also, your dog or cat at home probably isn't trying to impart any wisdom on your per say — unless it's possessed.  You'll know when you should look up the spiritual meaning of the animal  Your intuition will kick-in raising the flag to do so.

Here are some other animals (and their symbolic or spiritual meaning) that have "reached out" to give me guidance along this journey.  Remember, it doesn't just have to be a physical encounter.  Some animals will come to you through pictures, dreams, words, etc.  It's the frequency or amount that you see a particular animal that will trigger your noggin to look up the meaning.

## GRASSHOPPER:
When you see this guy, hop to it!  He brings you the courage the get projects done.  The grasshopper is also symbolic of "balance," so it's no surprise I've seen one a couple times on my journey.  Balance is crucial when it comes to completing tasks in life.  Too much on one side or the other and you start to lose focus.  Remember to make time for everything important and it'll all even out.

## GIRAFFE:
Despite the height, this animal is no tall tale.  The giraffe is symbolic of intuition and clairvoyance.  It lets you know the future.  Whatever you're predicting or manifesting is dead-on.  The long neck is especially symbolic of the "reach" it has — specifically with the reaching of certain goals that others can't.

## WOLF:
The wolf is a teacher.  When you see one, dig deep into your soul and learn more about the person you are and the person you're to become.  Stare down your fears and embrace the courage this animal brings.  The wolf is also about intuition —again, no surprise.

## SNAKE:
A very powerful totem! The snake is sharp! He will fine tune your intuition, bring about wisdom and conjure up even more creativity within you. Don't be afraid of the snake — it's your friend — and a friend for life. The snake is the symbol of eternity.

## OWL:
Who, What, When, Where and Why? All secrets and that which is hidden is revealed when the owl comes into your life. The term "wise like an owl" was coined for a reason. Listen to others by using the magic of the owl and you will learn "who's" your friend and "who's" not. The owl won't let you be deceived.

One final thought on animal totems. They can often bring about a theme. As you gather from mine, intuition is of high importance. The animals teach me to trust my gut and instincts about people. The spirit of the animal is always good. It is not there to deceive you. Even though I got a bad vibe from the crow — it wasn't the crow himself, rather the message he was trying to send. The crow was a faithful messenger. He just needed to get through to me in a way I'd understand. Make sense?

CHAPTER 9
# SOMETHING FISHY GOING ON

On countless weekends growing up, I would have to join my father and brother on our small fishing boat for what would seem like an endless expedition on one of the nearby Finger Lakes or on Lake Ontario. (**It's a Sign, Stupid!**) While the two of them would sit for hours fishing, I was trying to find anything possible to do on a boat. Needless to say, it wasn't easy. After all, I was surrounded by water. And, it was in Upstate NY so the idea that a band of pirates would come take me away wasn't even possible. Instead, I swam a lot. I tried fishing. It's not that it's hard; I just didn't care for it much. Aside from being boring as hell, there was something about a fish hooked by its mouth that rubbed me the wrong way. I felt bad for the fish — even though they would always be tossed back into the water.

This sentiment about fishing makes perfect sense to me now. I'm a Pisces. The fish. To this day, my brother still goes out fishing. He's an Aquarius — an air sign. My mother and father are both Libra — also an air sign. Looking back, this explains a lot growing up.

In the Zodiac, you are most compatible with signs that share your same element. Here's the breakdown:

| WATER | FIRE | AIR | EARTH |
|---|---|---|---|
| Pisces | Aries | Aquarius | Taurus |
| Cancer | Leo | Gemini | Virgo |
| Scorpio | Sagittarius | Libra | Capricorn |

This doesn't mean that you can't get along or be compatible with someone of another element. Air does fuel fire. Water is the salt of the Earth. We also all know that sometimes opposites attract. Plus, I'm a firm believer that love wins over all — including the Zodiac.

Given that I was a swimmer and absolutely love the water, it should come as no surprise that I look to the fish for daily guidance through my horoscope. I know there are many people who think it's a bunch of hogwash and intended for middle-aged woman with too much time on their hands. To those people, I say, why not try reading your horoscope for a week or two and see if you still have the sentiment toward it. If you ever want to know your future or how to proceed in certain situations, then the Zodiac may provide the guidance you're seeking. There are no coincidences in life. This doesn't mean that every time you open up the newspaper or go online to read your daily horoscope it will offer up some obvious and astounding astrological insight. The Zodiac speaks in "riddles," as my brother would say. You have to derive the meaning and apply it to your life. You have to think a little bit when using the stars for help. Also, the Zodiac will often offer up a scenario (depending on which source you use) meant to tell you things like "calm down," "watch your diet," "be nicer," etc. I think we can all agree that these aren't such bad things to keep in mind in life.

When I first moved to Las Vegas, I came into contact with a woman with whom I was in close friends for the next four years. However, when I initially met this woman, I got that stinging warm feeling my stomach and a voice popped into my head saying "You are going to have a huge blow-out fight." This was prior to knowingly being on my spiritual journey. So, I thought nothing of it and moved on. While I won't bore you with the incredible and jaw-dropping details of the big blow-out fight that indeed happened four years later — I will instead offer this up. The zodiac lets us get a glimpse of the future if you learn to use it correctly. I later learned that this woman is a Sagittarius. Sagittarius and Gemini are the two signs a Pisces must be careful of. They don't mix well. It doesn't mean I can't be friends with people of this sign. I have a couple good friends who are Gemini. Also, remember how opposites sometimes attract? Kristen Miranda who I mentioned a few chapters ago is a Leo — a fire sign. We get along famously despite water and fire being known for not mixing well.

As much as the Zodiac tells us who to surround ourselves with and who to avoid — it is also trying to tell us how to be more understanding. The Zodiac does not pit us against one another or try to create problems. It teaches you how to be a better human being. So, if you think it's a bunch of silliness — maybe approach it from the angle I just shared. Use it as a guide to become better in life. I think we can all agree that each of us can always use encouragement or a kick in the ass sometimes.

For those of you who want to dig deeper and investigate further with regard to your Zodiac sign, consider this. There are so many other factors that play into your sign. In other words, you can't look at it in generalities if you want to truly discover who you are and find your purpose in this world. Within each person there is a Sun Sign, a Moon Sign and a Rising Sign. Your combination of these three signs is sort of a caricature of you — a blue print of sorts. I'll quickly run through what each describes before I enlighten you to the gem of a creation that I am.

## SUN SIGN:
This is your basic blueprint -- your core.  The Sun changes once a month so it provides the most stability in any sign.  The Moon and Rising signs change quite frequently which is the reason two people under the same Zodiac sign can be so different from one another. The sun sign is representative of your personality.  When someone says "I'm a Pisces to tee," for example, these are the Sun Sign qualities he or she is referencing.  These are the basic attributes of the sign.

## MOON SIGN:
All about your insides — your sensitivity, the way you react to things and why you are who you are.  The Moon Sign is how you're built.  It is also your instinct and intuition.

## RISING SIGN:
Your rising sign is also known as your ascending sign.  They mean the same thing.  Your Rising Sign is what you shine to the world.  I always say that whatever is going on inside you — this is what you shine to the world.  Your rising sign is what you project and how people perceive you.  Your rising sign is tied directly to the precise time of day you were born.  So, whether you're an early bird or a *night owl* — with regard to the timing of your birth — makes all the difference in the world.

With that said, let's calculate.  I'll use myself as an example.  Before I do so, let me just give you some quick background and structure as to my make-up.  I'm a total dreamer who lives in two worlds — reality and non-reality.  Some might even say I'm from another planet.  If so, fine — take me to your leader as I have some questions to ask him or her.  I'm a writer, a thinker and a firm believer in the good of mankind.  I hate mean, non-compassionate people.  I'm the guy who wants to save the world.  While I'm an introvert in some ways, I'm the life of the party in public.  I have no filter — I say whatever is on my mind.  I will always lend a helping hand.  I'm grumpy, moody and a loner.  I need a lot of "me" time which is also "alone" time.  I have zero patience and ignorance is my mortal enemy. I can't make a decision to save my life unless it's urgent. In those situations, I can delegate and make decisions fearlessly. Pisces, in the Zodiac, is characterized by two fish swimming in opposite directions. This is very telling and eye opening. The trick in life is to get both fish swimming in the same direction — not working against one another. I look at it this way. The Pisces can be his or her own worst enemy at times. Also, I'm intuitive, altruistic, antagonizing and make "magic" happen.

So, if you take the day and time I was born, which is February 27th, 1976 at 5:21 in the Morning. I was born in Rochester, NY. By Astrological calculations, I am:

Sun Sign: Pisces
Moon Sign: Aquarius
Rising Sign: Aquarius

First off, that's a lot of damn water. Aquarius is symbolized by the water bearer even though it is an air sign. For that matter, that's a lot of air too! I frequently have to stop to remind myself to breathe. So what does this all mean?

## **MOON IN AQUARIUS**
Strongly opinionated, loves freedom, despises mediocrity, ignorance and incompetence, is original, smart, a loner, independent and surrounds him or herself with similar people. We are creators and therefore can easily reinvent ourselves from time to time. We tend to take on hobbies to escape from the world when need be. Remember, your moon sign reflects how you feel inside.

## **RISING IN AQUARIUS**
A person with Aquarius as his or her rising sign is one who values friendship. We are viewed as pieces of the overall

pie, if you will, when it comes to the world. On the positive side, people view us as gifted, creative, altruistic, likable, passionate and charitable. On the negative, we can be viewed as odd, eccentric, paradoxical, distant, disturbed, cold and utopian-minded. Again, your rising sign is what you shine to the world. It's how people view you.

So, with all that said, don't I sound like a dream date with a fucking disaster? Another way of putting it — I'm an enigma, wrapped in a conundrum that is perfectly packaged as a puzzle. There's also another way to decipher this wordy coding.

In the spiritual journey, you are on a mission to understand yourself, understand how you fit in with the world and figure out your purpose. You're trying to become better connected with the universe. If you don't know who you are inside, how can you achieve that? The Zodiac, particularly your moon and sun signs, help you understand who you are by nature — by default. Isn't this good information to know?

With regard to how other people perceive you — again; this is good information to have on hand. Think of it like a study done just for you. This study tells you your positive attributes, your negative and all those in between. Just because your rising sign tells you that you may appear "eccentric" to the world doesn't mean it will always be the case. Your rising sign is a great resource to help you see yourself through the eyes of another person. When you are truly able to do that, you can understand what you need to do to change. We all have work to do on ourselves. There's no shame in that. I doubt there's one person in the world who wouldn't want to become a better person if given the opportunity. Now, does the Zodiac seem so silly when you look at it from this perspective? In fact, I think it nicely fits in with the spiritual journey and would even say it's a necessary component.

# PART 4
# NOW YOU SEE ME

CHAPTER 10
# HAPPY BIRTHDAY

On Wednesday, February 20th 2013, while outside at work for fresh air and thinking, the woman who ran the front office (and her mouth far too much) came walking up to me. She informed me that I needed to be inside in 5 minutes as we would be cutting the cake to celebrate my 37th birthday. Just one tiny problem -- my birthday wasn't for another week. There I stood — looking intensely perplexed and awkwardly smiling — as co-workers gathered around to collect their piece of cake. Now, this was done deliberately. I mean, I filled out paperwork prior to starting the job (as we all do) that clearly indicated my date of birth. There were also 5 other Pisces oddly in the mix in this office — some of whom celebrated their birthday days before mine. I can't even make this up. Who does this? Better yet, why? (**It's a Sign, Stupid**)

The following week, on my birthday, I got a couple of "Happy Birthdays" from co-workers and one card. For the next several months, I kept racking my brain trying to figure this out. When you're in a spiritual journey, some odd things will happen. The Universe will put you in certain situations that appear strange to you. And, to the point where you scratch your head wondering what the hell is going on. Have this happen enough and you even start to wonder if you're going crazy. The good thing is, I wasn't. Once I interpreted what was going on, it made sense. Certain situations present themselves as the impetus to get you to look at other concepts that help you in your journey. Without the "situation" you might never think to look beyond to what it's ultimately trying to teach you. Now that you're scratching your head wondering what the hell I'm rambling on about, let me provide more clarity.

This particular situation opened my eyes to the concept of Mercury in Retrograde. Or, what I like to call the ruthless bitch that visits a few times a year — including right around my birthday in 2013. The universe was opening my eyes to a phenomenon that doesn't get a whole lot of attention. Mercury in Retrograde implies that for three weeks, this planet appears to be moving in reverse. As it appears to do this, so does your life. Here are the dates in case you'd also like to ponder why your life was a living hell during some predetermined weeks of 2013.

- February 23rd - March 17th
- June 26th - July 20th
- October 21st - November 10th

Now, look at these dates a little bit closer. Isn't it quite interesting that Mercury decides he'll create chaos during the months where all the water signs come to light. The first retrograde period falls when Pisces is predominantly active. The second falls when Cancer is predominantly active. The third period falls when Scorpio is predominantly active. When I first noticed this, I was a little awestruck. It's very eye opening. Now, don't be so quick to wipe your brow saying "Phew, glad I'm not a water sign." Your day will (or year for that matter) will come. Mercury works in retrograde — or backwards.

I hate to break it you Aquarius, but you and your fellow Air signs are next. That means Aquarius, Gemini and Libra will get the brunt of Mercury in Retrograde for the year 2014. However, Water signs aren't all in the clear just yet. There is some overlap of about a week where all Water signs will still be in the mix of these chaotic periods. Here are the dates for 2014:

- February 6th - February 28th
- June 7th - July 1st
- October 4th - October 25th

The concept of Mercury in Retrograde is nothing new. It's only new to people who've never heard it before. That means, for some, Mercury Retrograde will be a times of panic, displeasure or despair. For others, these will be times of reflection, learning and carrying on as normal. Remember, Mercury isn't just a planet. He's also the Greek "messenger" God. And, maybe he's trying to tell you something during these periods.

Fast forward to the tail end of June of 2013. No matter what I said to people, it was like they would do the complete opposite. If I said to someone, "Can we have a nice, calm talk," I would instead get a screaming match. Literally! I kid you not. It would drive me crazy. I had no idea why this was happening. Then my roommate shed some light on the situation. He told me that I was very difficult to figure out and needed to be more direct with my communication. "Nonsense," I said. I mean, I'm a communicator by nature — a broadcaster. I studied this in college. How could I possibly not be communicating effectively. (**It's a Sign, Stupid**)

To humor him, I conducted a little study. I would be extremely direct in my communication. Maybe even *overly* direct. Let's just say you would be amazed at the things you "think" someone knows, but doesn't, due to your communication not being direct enough.

There are a couple of other lessons and important notes about Mercury in Retrograde. These periods may not be best to make any big decisions, purchases or life altering choices. These periods, as my brilliant friend Adam explained, are sort of like the ebbs and flows in life. The ups and downs. And, although these periods present themselves during a specific Zodiac sign, that doesn't mean the rest of us are immune. These periods are only heightened for people of the particular sign the retrograde falls in.

Now that you know and understand how Mercury in Retrograde works, why not share it with someone else. It may make his or her life easier. You may open someone up to a concept that will give clarity and insight into an otherwise trying and seemingly impossible time. Not everyone will greet you with open arms regarding this concept. Some might even ask where you learned such a crazy idea and snarl at you. Should that happen — tell the person you learned it from a movie on Lifetime starring any number of washed-up child actors. Do not mention my name. I have a reputation to uphold. ;)

On another level, Mercury in Retrograde does give us opportunity. Rather than fight it, we can choose to allow our mind to be open to it as a way to learn and grow. Maybe there's a message in what seems like craziness taking place around us. If you can't come to a conclusion as to any sort of message — chalk it up to Mercury Retrograde. If anything, it's a great excuse to use when things just aren't going the way you planned!

## CHAPTER 11
# MANIFESTO!

It is here. We have arrived upon what is my favorite chapter in this book. Manifesto! What if I told you that you could have whatever you wanted in life just by believing or attracting it. Even more, what if I told you that whatever you dreamed of as a kid just may be directly correlated to what you receive later in life. I can unequivocally say that everything my mind thought of as a boy has come true later in life. And there's a secret to the process — one I didn't realize until recently. What if I said you also hold this power? That means, if you haven't experienced the same fate that I have, you still can. It's not too late. To better explain this, let me take you back in time to a younger Mike Doria.

About the age of 5 or 6, my Aunt and Uncle on my mother's side had given my brother, sister and I each a bench. They were small benches — sort of like stepping stools with an oval shaped top. What would seemingly be just an ordinary piece of furniture to a bigger toy collection — turned out to be one of the most important gifts I would ever receive. Each bench was made of wood and very nicely carved and shaped. The benches that my brother, sister and I received all had a different color wood. This made them identifiable as to whom they belonged. I can't remember for the life of me how my brother and sister interpreted their benches. After all, they were sort of an odd gift for kids. But I looked at mine as something bigger than what it was — a true stepping stool to propel me in life.

I remember putting my bench in front of the television. I would gather a stack of papers and place them on top of the bench. Then, I would find a pen and put that on top of the papers. I was prepared. The only problem, I wasn't so eloquent as a six year old. But it didn't matter. I would turn on the six o'clock news and watch the news anchors for a few minutes. Finally, I was ready. I would sit in front of the bench and pretend to deliver my own newscast. I'd be flipping through the pages and holding the pen just like the news anchors did. I remember this like it was yesterday. On one of my make-believe newscasts I began with the words "The who can man ran down the street." At 6 years old I didn't know how to read yet; I was learning this in Kindergarten. Sure, I could talk but my daily vernacular and conversation topics were hardly those of world affairs and local news. So, whatever worlds I learned kept making their way into the newscast. I was enamored by this — and clearly way ahead of my time. What kid does this?

As a kid, I also loved to draw and paint. These were gifts that were handed down through the genes of my predecessors. My Aunt Barb, for example, is a very skilled painter and craftswoman. Her paintings had a message and a unique point of view. She had a unique style. She also had a workshop, of sorts, downstairs in the basement of my grandparents' house. In fact, as you walk downstairs to the basement, the ceiling above the steps has a pretty sizable mural painted on it with very bright orange, green, yellow and pink colors. It caught my eye every time I was over to visit. I always admired my Aunt's artistic ability. It was just different and eye-catching. Also, out of practically anything, this woman could build a doll house that was incredible realistic and impeccable. All of this creative energy was enough to inspire me to paint and draw. I remember my mother had me sketch a couple of designs that would later be placed on some vases that she would make in her ceramics class. For a very long time in my childhood I had dream of becoming a Commercial Artist one day. If you also remember back to the TV show "Bewitched" — one of my all time favorites — Darren Stevens was a commercial artist. This only contributed to my inspiration of one day being in this career field.

And, as a child — I loved music. There was a piano in the living room of my grandparents' house. It was a standard, wooden upright piano that was generally out of tune. But, to a 7 year old — it sounded just fine. I would sit at that piano for quite a while singing and pounding on the keys as if I had any clue how to properly play. It didn't matter. In my mind, I was a musician. My improvised lyrics were magic. This wasn't my only exposure to music.

Also growing up, my parents would gather us kids in the living room on many Friday nights to listen to 45's on the record player. For you whippersnappers — a 45 is a smaller vinyl record that had one, maybe two songs on the front side and another on the back. And for you older folks who know what I'm talking about — remember the good old days?

As we sat in the living room, we would all sing along and sometimes dance. I know you're probably wondering what ridiculous Brady Bunch-like family does this. Mine! Some of the family favorites were anything written and recorded by the band Supertramp, Meatloaf or Neil Diamond. There was also a song that was quite overplayed called "Purple People Eater," by Sheb Wooley. This song actually reached number 1 on the Billboard Chart in the late 50's. It is also proof positive that the weirder you make things in life — I believe — the better the chance at commercial success. Don't ask me how I know this, it's just something I've picked up on in life. The song makes absolutely no sense. But I'll still listen to it and sing along to this day should I hear it. This friday night record playing would go on for a few years and was quite fun.

At one point, I wrote my first song as a kid. It didn't have music, naturally, as I was too young to really know how to play an instrument. "Playing in the Rain," was the name of the song. I took it to my parents to show them. It didn't go very far. Remember, I was the middle child. Ignored -- with a capital "I." But, bear with me. This constant ignoring actually leads to bliss. I swear.

Now as I got a little bit older — right about 12 or 13 years old, I had somehow figured out how to rig a make-shift recording studio in the bedroom my brother and I had shared. We had moved from an upstairs bedroom to the downstairs family room that my father had converted into one big bedroom. This giant bedroom would later become two smaller bedrooms divided by wall. We each needed our own space as we got older. It was certainly a process in my household - with anything!

So, after mysteriously learning how to rig up a recording studio, complete with small microphones and other stereo equipment received as a birthday gift from my Uncle, I began singing along with my cassette tapes of other artists and recording voice in with their track. This is where I first learned to sing — and it did take a lot of practice. This is also where I developed the gift of listening — closely. Beware! Don't ever tell my anything that you want me to forget. I remember everything. (**It's a Sign, Stupid!**) This of course is a gift in some ways and a curse in others.

On the gift end, learning how to listen — especially to what the universe is trying to tell you — is hugely important for growth both personally and spiritually. Knowing what to listen for is equally as important. Do you ever have one of those moments where someone says something and you immediately go "What did you say?" Or, maybe you've been standing in line and two people chatting behind you say something that make your ears perk up? Maybe you're watching a movie and one of the lines an actor or actress says jumps out at you forcing you to think about it. Maybe you're at a concert or a Broadway show and a particular song or scene piqued your interested or curiosity. That is the Universe trying to tell you something. That is the Universe asking you to pay attention to what was just said. Recognize this enough times and you'll realize the Universe is trying to train your ears. With each instance this happens, the Universe is trying to get your attention focused on something very specific. It could be some useful advice for the long-haul or some imparted wisdom for the short term. You'll know when these instances arise. Don't ignore or dismiss. You never know what you may be missing out on. God has a unique way of using friends, family, actors, singers and perfect strangers to convey a message meant for your ears.

On the curse end, you have no idea how many times I've had people say "I never said that," to which I have to beg to differ and get inwardly aggravated because arguing is these instances is useless.

Now back to my childhood. I loved pretending I was a news reporter, wanted to be a commercial artist while growing up and developed an intense love of music. Creativity was in my blood and genes. And, when you're the middle child who was ignored quite a bit — you tend to finely tune this creativity. You also end up with a larger than life imagination. Nothing is outside the realm of possibility — nothing! And that, my friends, is one truly magical childhood.

Think about it. I somehow manifested myself into a TV News Reporter. When I left that business and became a Marketing professional, I found myself designing all sorts of electronic emails, flyer, banners — even my own book cover. That sounds a lot to me like a Commercial Artist. But wait — what about music? Well, guess what I'll be pursuing — even further — very shortly to complete this little trilogy I wished into my life at a very young age? How powerful is that?

How cool is that? And, yet, I'm not the only one with this ability. You have it too. You just have to know how to tap into it. And, It's still your lucky day because I'm going to tell you how.

First things first, stop being such an adult about everything. I know that runs contrary to what we're taught and what's expected of us as we get older. But, there are exceptions to the rules. Kids have a unique energy about them and look at the world through rose-colored glasses. They're not bogged down by the mundane or exhausting day to day that adults must endure. They're happy. They believe. They're magical. Tap into your inner kid from time to time. You'll be amazed at what comes your way. You must truly believe though. Remember what I said in an earlier Chapter regarding the tendency of minds to gravitate toward the negative. You must fight this in order to manifest.

Ok, kiddo — here's the next part. You must learn how to use the Law of Attraction. Now, I can already hear some of you say "Not this psycho-babble bullshit again." Sorry, Charlie! It's true. The law of attraction is one of the most powerful concepts and forces in the Universe. Everyone has the ability to attract what he or she wants. The timing is a whole different story. God will give you what you want and need when it's time. This doesn't mean give up. It just means have patience. I've figured out that attracting what you want does require some learning. Maybe it's a lesson. Maybe it's a spiritual and metaphoric instructional pamphlet teaching you how to properly use this power and whatever it is you're trying to attract. You can't just attract what you want for simple pleasure or take it for granted. I also wouldn't count on wishing for lumps of gold or unicorns. I mean, really? But, you can ask for money. And, I'm going to tell you how to do that in the next chapter.

Careful what you wish for! I don't mean that in a negative way. I use it as a way to segue into another very important part of manifesting or wishing. I was recently chatting with Adam (the same Adam I mentioned in an earlier chapter). He was given rather short notice from his boss that he had to deliver an eight minute speech in front of a wider group of co-workers. About an hour or two before delivering his short speech, he said he got nervous, anxious and maybe a touch doubtful about whether he could pull it off. In other words, that little voice in all of us that somehow screams rather loudly saying things like "we can't" or "we're not good enough" or "we're incapable." When Adam, finally regained control over that voice he went into his speech with confidence, nailed and was greeted with accolades for a job well-done afterward. Then came the gem that Adam is even better at delivering. He said why be afraid of a speech? It was part of the territory. He had manifested that position at work that came with that responsibility. He attracted it.

I believe that once you're in tune with Universe, God won't put you in situations you can't handle. That doesn't mean you can "wing" it so to speak. You have to put in some effort. This, of course, is true of anything in life.

No part of me believes whatsoever that I didn't manifest my career choices from an early age. I suppose what isn't yet clear is why at such a young age "work" was so important. Sure, as kids we all say that we want to be an astronaut or a police officer or nurse, etc. But, my choices were very specific. There are pieces of the puzzle in the spiritual journey that take time to figure out. In other words, I don't have all the answers and much more learning is ahead. This is learning that I embrace and fully look forward to. But, I can find some solace in something that has bothered me my entire life and something with which I am starting to understand. Middle Child Syndrome! And, here's where you come in if you are a middle child.

While on the phone with my dad one day I flat out told him how I felt — ignored and unimportant. He told me that he thought about that a lot and felt badly. He also told me that I was a good kid who got good grades and didn't require a lot of guidance, etc. I told him that while that made sense, I still needed a father. He agreed. But, then I shared something else with him — the positive side. Yes, there is a positive side to being a middle child. Instead of staying stuck in that mindset, I began looking at being the middle child as a blessing. I learned how to rely on myself in life, provide for myself, become creative and run with my dream and vision. I figured out how to reach for the stars — and grab tightly. I'm not the statistic I once thought. I'm a success story. And, I'm proud of that — and myself. I'm humbled by it and I'm thankful for it. Had I not been the middle child, who knows where I would be in life. I may not have become a news reporter. I may not have fought as hard as I did to make something of myself in life. I may never have come into my power. God really does work in mysterious ways to awaken us to our potential.

If you're a middle child who was ignored, consider altering your viewpoint of this circumstance. Find the beauty in it. Find the strengths this helped you gain. In doing so, I think you just might find some peace and new found path from which you can grow into an even more amazing human being. If you are the parent of a middle child and you suspect you may not have been there enough for him or her — it's not too late. Pick up the phone and tell your son or daughter that you love him or her and are a proud parent. This will go further than you suspect and have such a profound positive impact on your relationship.

## CHAPTER 12
## EYE OF NEWT

"The money really starts to come in at 37," said the palm reader. I was sitting at a table among aspiring actors and actresses. I was doing some background acting in the movie "Burt Wonderstone." (**It's a Sign, Stupid**) I never really had — and still don't for that matter — any ambition of being an actor. It was more a way to earn a little extra cash while transitioning into my new career. I was 35 years old. I'm a total believer in what others see as fairytale hocus-pocus. I'll explain why in a minute. I didn't seek out this seer. She was put in front of me for a reason. Looking back on it, I also find it amusing and perfectly logical that she came while sitting on the set of a movie about a struggling Las Vegas magician.

After sharing my fate, I spent the next year and a half periodically thinking about what she had said. I wondered why 37 was the age when this "jackpot" of sorts would come into play. About three months out from 37, I noticed a shift in my bank account. In addition to my full-time job, some other opportunities had come my way. My editor who I spent several years working under at one magazine jumped ship for another. After asking me to switch-over three times, I finally said yes and began working under her again. For whatever reason — the third time in life really is my charm. If someone tells me something for a third time, asks me something for a third time — that's when I really pay attention even more closely. I've come to realize it's the Universe trying to send me a message. It's never failed me. Switching magazines brought much more work opportunity.

And, the work is something I thoroughly enjoy. About this time, I had also started getting some requests to do some freelance writing and marketing for businesses. I had done this previously, but all pro bono as I wanted to get more experience. Recognizing I was ready — and perhaps on the verge of something bigger — I decided to start my own PR & Marketing small business. I got a business license in January — just a little under two months away from my birthday.

As I blew out the candles on my cake on my 37th birthday, I thought to myself "man, these candles have it easy." They were only burning on one end. I was burning the candle at both ends. I had a full-time job, a freelance gig and small business. I also had bags the size of Jupiter under my eyes. About a week later, I thought back to what the fortune teller told me. "Wow," I said. She was right. For the first time in my life, I was actually making decent money. Granted, three jobs were necessary to bring in this money, but the palm reader never said how —just "when" it would happen. So there I was working 10 times harder than I ever had before. But then another thought popped into my head. Remember what I said last chapter about meeting the Universe half way? I believe that's exactly what I did. Take it from me — learning how to juggle this new lifestyle and finding any kind of balance was difficult. I spent many nights aggravated — some even in tears. I was completely overwhelmed. Luckily, as I mentioned in Chapter 7, Holly Madison showed me what I needed to learn to strike this balance.

You can attract whatever you want in life — the good and the garbage. Do the right things and the right things will come. Do the wrong things and the wrong results will prevail. It's just that simple. Don't dismiss opportunity because it seems too overwhelming or impossible. Give it a shot. You never fail in life until you give up. You may fail several times but that doesn't mean you're done. The

Universe handed me this work situation for a reason. I was meant to learn something from the experience. And, that I did! Marry someone with gobs of money so I can sit on my fat ass and do nothing. I'm teasing. The first lesson was a revelation about me.

Let's begin with the revelation and a little story about the person for whom this book is fully dedicated. My Aunt El. El is short for Elena — pronounced *el-en-uh*. This name was given to her in honor of who would've been my Great Aunt Elena who died either prior to birth or very shortly thereafter. I learned this while chatting with my Grandmother just a couple months before she passed away. She died New Year's Day 2006. She knew her time was near, but kept saying she wanted to live to see the New Year. She was a determined Italian woman and she got her way. As a young kid, I put my Aunt El through torture when she babysat. I kid you not — there was not a wooden spoon to be found in a kitchen drawer at any relative's house. All were used to knock some sense into me when I would open my big mouth. And, I kid you not, every single wooden spoon somehow snapped in half when it would meet my ass. This became a running joke in the family as I grew older. It was bizarre. As a kid, I also developed a nickname for my Aunt El. You ready for this doozy that came out of my mouth right around age six? "**Auntie Fat Ass!**" Yup! I was just darling as a kid. I remember the day I first called her that — screaming it out the bedroom window after being sent to my room. Now, this has become somewhat of a term of endearment later in life. While, I don't call her that anymore, she got a kick out of the whole story and reminds me all the time of the little snot I was at an early age. She also changed it to "**Auntie Phat Ass**" to give it a much nicer connotation. I should also point out, she's not even "fat." That just happened to be the first thing that came out of my mouth at that particular moment. But, I must have learned that language somewhere — right Aunt El? Hint -- hint. My Aunt El is also my Godmother, as you learned back in Chapter 1. Somewhere along the line, she had revealed to the family that she was a Witch. No; not the broom flying kind, the normal kind. The kind connected to the Universe and uses her gifts for good. She is a palm reader and can see the future. I'll tell you why I know this in just a minute. Now, you have to know that upon hearing this news, the jokes started flying. When over for dinner; I would tease and ask if she had added "Eye of Newt," to the pasta boiling on the stove. Even as an adult, I still an uncanny ability for being a smart-ass. "Keep laughing," she'd say.

Right before I moved across the country, she had a friend read my tarot cards. (**It's a Sign, Stupid**) What I remember the most is the "sun" being prevalent in this reading. In part, I believe it was indicative of the desert I was about to dwell and the abundance of sunshine. Another way to decipher this — the "light" this move would bring. It was also to serve as a reminder that I was a Pisces — a water sign. Leaving my hometown that sits on a Great Lake for a city smack dab in the middle of desert seemed a little interesting. I was a fish out of water of sorts. But, my job was to find the water in the desert. The last thing my Aunt El said to me prior to my departure was "I hope you're not moving to run away from your problems." I will never forget this. I wasn't sure what she had meant. I wasn't running — I was chasing my dream. I was furthering my career. I've come to learn that her statement wasn't to be taken so literally — necessarily. Instead, it was a sneak peek into the future — a future she saw.

As I pointed out in the prologue, Las Vegas isn't the easiest of cities to live. You meet all sorts of oddballs left and right. A friend said it best. If you live in Vegas for three years or more — you've earned your stripes. You can live anywhere. This city is not for the weak. I've had three friends die in the seven years. I've had friends run for this hills and get the hell out of dodge as quickly as possible. As former Las Vegas Mayor Oscar Goodman once told me, this is the city of second chances. Mayor Goodman is one of the most intriguing and inspiring people I've met in Las Vegas. And, his words are 100 percent true. This city affords people the chance to leave their old life behind and reinvent a new one from practically scratch. Mayor Goodman and I have spoken many a times. Why were those particular worlds the ones I remember so well? Think back to what I said last chapter. The Universe gives you messages through other people sometimes. You have to learn when to recognize this is happening.

My Aunt El's parting words made perfect sense. She was giving me a tiny bit of information about my future and some wise advice regarding what *not* to do should the going get tough. Run. Right after I left TV news, I was going to move to Texas and stay with my brother and sister-in-law for a little while. Both were in the military at the time. Naturally, I told my family back home of my plans. My Aunt El said she didn't think moving was a good idea and to stay put. I didn't pay much attention to it.

At my going away party, as my band was performing what would have been our last gig, I got that warm stinging feeling in stomach again. It was my intuition. And this time, it was more powerful than it had ever been. Enough so that it literally paralyzed me for a few seconds this time. It was so powerful, I didn't dare dismiss it. I got on the microphone and told everyone that I was staying in Las Vegas. About a month later, my brother and sister-in-law were reassigned by the military and moved to their new post in Virginia. I would have been stuck in Texas with no job, no family and no place to live.

After the "going away party," I really started to think about what my Aunt said. How could she know all this? The answer is simple. There really are Witches or people who have unique powers and ability on this planet. As I previously mentioned — I always had a fascination with the show "Bewitched," growing up. I was also a fan of the show

"Charmed" too which documented the life of three sister witches who worked together against evil. (**It's a Sign, Stupid!**) As I pointed out — words really do have power. Think about it. Someone's words can build a person up or cut someone down. Words can save lives — and end them just the same. The words we choose can put a person in the greatest of moods — or the worst. The words we speak can blossom friendships or force a parting of ways.

On the spiritual end, people reach out to God or the Universe in times of need or dire straits. People also reach out to God and the Universe to give praise and thanks when times are good. Prayer is a very common practice. A witch's spell is nothing more than a prayer. They're uniquely connected to the Universe and have the ability to ask it for very particular outcomes. Much like we do in prayer. Any decent witch would know not to abuse this gift and use it for evil — much like we don't ask God to be inhumane or create havoc in peoples' lives.

My Aunt's words to me regarding running away from problems were a sign — a foreshadow. When Vegas got tough — and it got rough for a while — I didn't run. I instead found a spiritual journey that has made life an incredible adventure filled with all sorts of wonder and eye-opening experiences. Don't dismiss a witch, palm reader or tarot card reader. Instead, open up your heart and mind a bit. Life really is as a much a magical experience as it is one of logic.

Just prior to writing this book, I had started to give some real thought about moving to Los Angeles. When chatting with my Aunt El, she said that my time in Las Vegas was still not done. I didn't question it. When I told her that I was also thinking about writing a children's book based on a "vision" I had, her response was "write the other book first." Now, how the hell could she know (**It's a Sign, Stupid!**) would be written if she weren't a bonafide Witch? I also told her that I had the feeling that I'm supposed to help people — almost as a Therapist. I went on to tell her that I would need a license to do so and didn't want to go back to school to get another degree. "Why do you need a degree," she said. From there, she got me to open my eyes once again. I could very well be a therapist and help people through my gift — writing. You don't need a license to write a book. As I once said in a blog post — we are all singers, actors, dancers and artists in life. You just have to perform from the stage you are meant.

**Thank you "Auntie Phat Ass," for your magical wisdom and support. I owe you the world for encouraging me to stay in Las Vegas so this book would see the light of day. I love you!**

Back to the work situation the Universe handed me following the fortune teller's prediction. This taught me another lesson. Working at the rigorous pace I did left little time to play and even less time enjoy life — or so I thought. As much as the palm reader predicted this future for me, there were parts of it that were up to me to discover. The discovery I made is that you must take time out to simply enjoy what's around you. The work will get done — no matter how many jobs you work. Thank you to the Universe for this important lesson. While I still work very hard to achieve and accomplish all I want to do in life — I now make time for family, friends and charity. **Now you see me.** The "me" the Universe had intended. Odd, isn't it, the situations we're put in to come to a particular realization. Sometimes it takes a well-choreographed and unique Universal plan for it all to sink in.

# PART 5
# NEW GUY

## CHAPTER 13
# NUMBERS GAME

It was like I was being given a code to crack. Yet, I couldn't seem to figure it out. It drove me crazy for 6 months. No matter where I went, I would start seeing numbers. They were significant numbers. And, it wasn't like any other confrontation with numbers I had seen in the past. This time, it was as if they were trying to tell me something. I was knowingly on the spiritual journey — so I knew something had to be up. (**It's a Sign, Stupid**) The most prominent of numbers: 2-27 in that order. This is the month and day of my birthday. The numbers 23, 3, 9-11, 7, 13 also stuck out. What the hell could this mean? I had no idea. None! But there was some importance to the numbers I was seeing.

23 is a number I always place a chip on when playing roulette. I gamble maybe 3 times a year and never spend more than $40 dollars when I do. If I lose the $40, I stop. If I win, I keep playing a little longer but never press my luck. The number 23 was a bet that was born out of an inside joke, but one that proved to turn up rewards time and time again. 3 is significant due to a Las Vegas trip several years

prior to moving to the city. I had spent all of my money and had about a week before I would get another paycheck. In your mid 20's, as a news reporter, it's very common to live paycheck to paycheck. The money in this field is not the greatest unless you're an anchor or news reporter in a top 10 market. Also, managing money wisely in my mid 20's wasn't among my strong suits. So, I had taken my last few chips, placed them all on the number 3 and crossed my fingers that the ball would end up in that slot. I was at Paris Hotel on vacation with my roommate at the time. Jackpot! The dealer hit the 3 and I was afloat until work handed out my next paycheck. I never forgot that moment. 9-11, as we all know, is a very sad and significant day in American history. 7 is the number I considered to be my lucky number. 13 is the day in October my father was born and it's also the number of the station I had worked at in Rochester - Channel 13 news.

I would get that warm, stinging feeling in my stomach when I started to notice these numbers. It didn't stop there. I would start to see them on receipts, license plates while driving, mixed into phone numbers, on billboards and all in such a way that I would take particular notice. What the hell was the universe trying to tell me? This literally went on for six months before I finally got aggravated and decided to investigate.

When it happened for the final time before being enlightened as to the meaning — I decided to search the internet to arrive at a conclusion. It couldn't hurt, right? I didn't even really know what to type into the search box. I don't even recall what I typed exactly. I just remember something along the lines of numbers and code, etc. When I hit return, it was like the heavens opened, light hit me in the face and the angels voices echoed. This crazy combination I'd been trying to figure out was none other than Numerology. To help better explain what this is all about, you may want to visit the website www.numerology.com.

If you don't know anything about Numerology, or are even weirded out by the thought of it — so was I, at first. I mean, who wouldn't be? But, the reporter in me — that didn't just go away when I'd left that career — came out and started to do some investigating into this unfamiliar territory. Much like your social security number which uniquely identifies you among the masses of people, so does your birth date when it comes to Numerology. Even more — your birth name is also a code of sorts that will provide you with one hell of a road map for life. Grab a pen and paper because you're about to find out your life path number — a very important number to know. I'll use my birth date as an example. The trick is to add the numbers and break them down into one single number. But, as with anything in life— there are some weird rules. My birth date is 02-27-1976. Use your full birth year. Moving left to right add the numbers together. My birthday, when added, results in the number 2005. Break it down to just one number by adding again. 2 + 0 + 0 + 5 = 7

02 + 27 + 1976 = 2005
2+0+0+5 = 7

LIFE PATH NUMBER: 7

Let's do another birth date just to provide another example. You're in luck whoever was born on October 14th, 1993 because I'll do the work for you.

10 +14 + 1993 = 2017
2+0+1+7 = 10
1 + 0 = 1

LIFE PATH NUMBER: 1

Again, you always want to add until you come to the lowest number possible. The exception to the rule is when you arrive at one of three master numbers 11, 22 and 33. Don't break them down further to 2, 4 and 6 respectively. If you possess one of these master numbers, you're kind of a special case. You get some extra insight into your life and how to figure out your place in this world. According to www.numerology.com, 11 is associated with instinct and reserved for psychics, clairvoyants and prophets. 22, according to the Website is considered to be the most powerful number and nicknamed "The Master Builder" number. And, 33 — according to the site is the "mover and shaker" of master numbers and nicknamed "The Master Teacher."

So what do these numbers mean? Well, let's analyze the "7," my life path number. The "7," is the incessant seeker of truth and Truth with a capital "T" who is concerned with the mysteries of life. This person is often loner (as my Zodiac sign suggests), and has a unique view of the world. The "7" also needs to learn balance. Sounds a lot like me huh? I'm on a spiritual journey. I believe in magic and power and manifestation. And balance, as you learned from Chapters 7 & 11 is my weak point. What does your life path number say about you?

Now, you may read your life path number and think to yourself "this doesn't really sound like me." Here's my take on this. Some may agree, others may not — but this is my perception based on personal experience in the spiritual journey. Since your particular life path number encompasses everyone else who shares that life path number, you may not display all of the traits associated. Another way to look at it — especially with some of the negative traits — maybe you've learned to overcome those negative traits. After all, numerology is here to help and point out areas for which we each need to improve in life. It also tells you the areas for which you'll have the most success.

Just as you birth date provides some insight into your spiritual and personal DNA, so does your name. In numerology, your name and its meaning are calculated a little bit differently as there are numbers assigned to the letters. I would encourage everyone to get a hold of their Primary Life Chart. There are numerous places online to get your chart. I particularly like Carol Adrienne and her Website www.caroladrienne.com. When I ordered my chart and began reading, I was all out flabbergasted. While in some ways it provided details I already knew; it also gave me very important nuggets of information that serve as cornerstones to my being. The chart is very detailed. It provides both your lifelong analysis and also gives you a yearly overview. How interesting is it to know that each year we can get a detailed chart that will tell us how to proceed for maximized success. Let's look at some specifics in my chart. We'll start with my name. My first middle name is that of my father and paternal grandfather. My second middle name is that of my maternal grandfather. I was given two middle names because my mother was sure she would have more kids after I was born. She had miscarried twice prior to getting pregnant with my sister. Therefore, she and my father wanted to be sure these names were passed along. When my brother arrived — just 11 months after I did, he took my maternal grandfather's middle name - Joseph. My brother and I are considered "Irish Twins." For two weeks out of the year, we are the same age.

Michael Ferdinand Joseph Doria

Michael = 33 **(master number)** meaning "Master Healer or Master Teacher"
Ferdinand = 3 meaning "Communicator"
Joseph = 1 meaning "Leader"
Doria = 11 **(master number)** meaning "Master Intuitive" and "Inspirer"

My name, according to my chart gives me great sensitivity to artistic details, light, beauty, harmony and the feelings of others. My destiny, according to the chart is **"Uplifter"**

If you're on the fence with regard to your belief in this, allow me to blow your mind. According to my chart from www.caroladrienne.com, it says:

*"You must bring the qualities of your Birth Path to your Destiny as a Generator of Positive Ideas, a Communicator, Motivator, and Creative Specialist in Arts/Music/Drama. KEY: Develop your talent for speaking, writing, color, salesmanship, entertainment and children's activities. CAREERS: Sales & Marketing, Toy Design, Graphics, TV Actor, Publishing, Sports, Fashion, Teaching, Florist, Cosmetics, Model."*

My personality, according to my chart is to be authentic. The word authentic is HUGE in my spiritual journey and speaks directly to my inclination as a life path 7 to seek out truth. My habit challenge is to learn to be compassionate. My specific birth day — the 27th is associated being "Spiritual," according to the chart with a vision for love, tolerance and peace. My birth path is described as "Catalyst," and tells me that I must use *intuition* to understand the message in the moment.

Given everything I've shared and discussed in this book thus far — this chart is dead on. It is incredible. I've given a six other people their chart as an experiment to see if they would come to the same conclusion regarding its veracity. All concur, it's accurate. What's even more amazing is the process by which I came to discovering this chart. Those particular numbers that I kept seeing are all sprinkled into this chart. The 7, 3, 11, 9 and 27. There is absolutely no way this is coincidence. None whatsoever!

Recall what I pointed out just two chapters ago regarding my career choices. It seems to me I accomplished several on that list. God is leading me to music. I will answer his calling — in fact, God has made it loud and clear that this is what I must do. How do I know? Let me offer up another story.

I have a unique knack for losing my keys. (**It's a Sign, Stupid**) If I added up the amount of time spent looking for misplaced keys, I would probably be sick to my stomach. When I purchased my latest car, I didn't even have it for two months before I had already lost the keys. I still haven't found them. I'm using a spare set. I remember setting them on the floor near my bedroom door when I became distracted and preoccupied with a matter that needed attention downstairs. When I returned — they were gone. I have no idea where they went. If you ask me, they magically disappeared because I have searched my room high and low to no avail. It's like they got up and walked away. For several months this bothered me. I mean, keys don't just get up and walk away. However, it all clicked one day. While the keys are still lost — their MIA status was supposed to capture and focus my attention on something else. Though my name is Michael, I go by the nickname "Mike." Only family members call me by my full name. A few of my friends call me "Mikey." I got thinking about this one day while knowingly on my spiritual journey. "Mikey" sounds a lot like "My Key." A few years ago I bought a guitar. While I can play a little guitar, I feel very awkward with it. As a kid, I played the clarinet. As an adult, I sing, write lyrics left and right and can play a little flute and a little guitar. Then it hit me — take piano lessons! How did I come to this conclusion. "My Key," and constantly losing my keys were a sign leading me to piano keys. I went out and bought a keyboard and am learning piano. Remember how I said the Universe will find a very unique way of you getting you to come to a realization? There are only two chapters of this book remaining. I hope you're starting to come to some "key" conclusions of your own.

## CHAPTER 14
## FIX-O, CHANGE-O REARRANGE-O

On a rather chilly and rainy day in Rochester, NY I was assigned to cover none other than a shooting that had taken the life of a man. As my photographer and I turned onto the street where the victim lived, I did what any reporter would do — took a deep breath and crossed my fingers. Then, I got out of the car and knocked on the front door. When a woman answered, I had just enough time to explain who I was and ask for an interview before being met with a rather loud "NO." She then slammed in my face. This happens quite a bit in news reporting. It's comes with the territory. What happened next isn't necessarily common. In fact, it's brazen. When that door closed, some force came over me. I opened the door, walked right into entry way and yelled "LISTEN TO ME." She turned around. (**It's a Sign, Stupid!**) I quickly changed my tone and apologized for the loss of her son. "I'm not like other reporters — I actually care," I said. I went on to explain that I didn't want all the attention surrounding her son's death to go to the person accused of taking his life. I further explained that her late son deserved some attention and air-time too. "Please; tell me a little bit about him and the kind of person he was." For the next five minutes, that woman gave me an on-camera interview and photo of her son to use on the evening news. She helped me, but I also helped her. I changed her perception of a "News Reporter.

I'm sure you're familiar with the phrase "Perception is Reality." It's a phrase by which I'm bothered. The main reason being — it doesn't necessarily get to the truth. It is usually a one-sided and narrow-minded conclusion. After all, a perception is just that - a perception. It's an excuse to ignore the truth and avoid further investigation. It's an excuse that also exonerates us from any responsibility. Consider this. Let's say, for example, that person "A" perceives person "B" to be difficult to work with. Person "B" believes that he or she is just trying to do the best job possible. Which person is right and which is wrong? Neither!

Wouldn't it seem fairer if person "A" would change his or her perception of person "B" and try to see the positive attributes? In doing so, person "A" just might come to understand person "B" for the hard-working and determined individual that he or she is. And, person "B" isn't off the hook. Providing that he or she knows this perception exists, some action should be taken to remedy his or her reputation. Both people have to do some bending and shifting when it comes to their thinking. After all, we're taught as kids to always put ourselves in someone else's shoes to understand various viewpoints. In my opinion — and I'm just as guilty sometimes — we often forget this concept as adults. Furthermore, why do we teach our kids one thing and do just the opposite?

As adults, we have so much power and opportunity to fix so many problems that persist in this world. If we truly practiced what we preached, wouldn't our daily lives be a bit easier? What's even more interesting is how often we revert back to a fourth grade mentality and play the blame game. We draw lines in the sand, pick sides and fail to take any responsibility for our actions. It's someone else's fault. It's someone else who is the problem. We must stop this. We are all at fault. But, we are all the solution at the same time. How can parents seriously expect to teach their kids to be understanding when that kid spends his or her formative years watching his or her parents do just the opposite? How can we expect our youth to learn to comprise and come to solutions when adults refuse to do this on a daily basis? Kids are not dumb. They pick up on the habits of adults. This leads to the perpetuation and exacerbation of an awful cycle.

How many times have you been asked whether you would go back in time to change a particular situation if given the opportunity? All of us have said "yes" at one point or another. What's interesting is it's the only angle or viewpoint from which we're often willing to look. First of all, if we were given the power or ability to go back in time — changing anything would change everything.

Let's say you time traveled back in time to 1998 just for fun. While there, you decide to pick a very beautiful flower from a garden in front a person's house. When you return to the present with the hope of putting that beautiful flower in a water-filled vase — not everything would be as it was when you left. Think about it. Your flower picking came with some consequences. What if that flower would've been the inspiration for a little girl walking to school to bring out her artistic ability? What about the person who planted it? With it gone the next day, this person is standing out front scratching his or her head wondering where it went. Up walks the mailman and the two start chatting. Along comes a driver who loses control of the car, jumps the curb and kills both the mailman and person who planted the flower. This widely known phenomenon whereby the future is changed by manipulating the past is known as the Butterfly Effect. Though impossible to time travel like that, it would be too risky to change the past.

But, we do know from experience, that history repeats itself. Agreed? This is especially true of wars, economic downturns, etc. So, if history repeats itself — then we should really be changing the future to fix problems. If we can better control the future, we wouldn't have to "imagine" going back in time to fix mistakes and problems. Many of these problems wouldn't exist in the first place. Now, this may sound very utopian — and it is in a sense. But, we have to start somewhere, right? The great part is we all scriptwriters of the future. We all have the ability to leave our impression. And, if we started making some better decisions; future generations would have a better blueprint from which to work. This is the side we should be looking toward. This is the power we should all be harnessing. Even on a personal level, we all have the ability to write ourselves a better future that will start to wipe away problems. Our attitudes toward people could be tuned-up. Our behaviors — some of which cause a wave of consequences — could be curbed. Slowly, but surely, we eventually start to erode some of the foundation and basis of many of life's problems.

Consider this example. How many times have you walked by a plastic bag, cup or other piece of trash that was lying on the ground? Countless times! As have I. While excuses may vary as to why any one of us didn't think to pick it up and dispose of it properly; the bottom line is — that piece of trash remains as litter. You might be thinking that one person picking up a piece of trash would hardly end littering as we know it. And, you're right — if you allow that perception to be reality and persist. I challenge you to consider another viewpoint. Let's say person "A" notices the cup or bag lying on the ground, picks it up and tosses it into a nearby trash can. From an apartment window, person "B" sees what person "A" just did. This moves person "B" to start picking up a piece of someone else's litter on occasion to properly dispose it. Person "C" just saw person "B" do this while looking out the window of the bus he or she was riding. Person "C" is now moved by this — and you see where this is going. Sooner or later, the littering problem isn't much of a problem anymore.

Now, I fully realize the amount of years and lifetimes over this may take to fully correct. Does that mean we should throw up our hands because we won't have to worry about it? It'll be the problem of generations yet to be born? Well, what if people living back in the 1800's had this foresight or practiced this idea. I'm not assigning blame — I'm just merely using them as an example. We would currently be living in a society that has fewer problems and issues — no? You may not live to see the fruits of this particular labor, but you would die knowing that you were part of the greater solution. Is that better than dying realizing you did little to protect and help future generations? I may also add these future generations, in many cases, are comprised of your own bloodline. These are your children's children and so on.

It's about time we all flip our script, change our perceptions and learn to get along better. The world depends on it. Future generations depend on it. We must teach our kids better and walk the talk we talk. We talk a big game. But we also all know that actions speak louder than words. Who's in?

CHAPTER 15
## WE ALL FALL DOWN

The trick is getting back up. It's not easy. But it's a necessity. While driving my friend Mike home one evening — the same Mike you were introduced to way back in chapter One — we were having a deep discussion about life. We would do this from time to time. It was very therapeutic and very interesting. We were connecting and learning from one another. We were gathering new insight and new viewpoints from our exchange of words with one another. I could sit and talk about the world, my beliefs, and passions until the day is done. I could sit and talk with you about yours too. This is what makes me tick. Out of this comes understanding. Out of conversations comes ideas. Out of ideas come solutions and hope. On this particular car ride he said to me "I admire your ability to pick yourself back up and keep fighting when you're down." He went to talk about how I may get deflated at times, but never defeated. (**It's a Sign, Stupid**) I'll never forget these words. He's right. This is my M-O in life. It's not an easy one to rely on at times due to the severity of any given situation; but I try. I came to Las Vegas at the top of my game. A few years later, I was at rock bottom trying to keep my head afloat. I'm back, or at least like to think I am, at the top of my game again. But I didn't resurface without a lot of soul-searching, internal digging and emotional redecorating. I blame myself for 90 percent of all that hasn't gone quite as I had planned in life. There are so many instances where I could have done better. There are countless times I could have behaved differently. There are zillions of times where I could have chosen my battles more wisely. But I'm human.

I've been thinking a lot lately in this journey about myself. I know that sounds completely self-centered and maybe even teetering on egotistical. But hear me out. How can we become better people if we don't become self centered. Being self-centered at times is not the same as being selfish. In fact, it leads to becoming selfless. If asked to put together a presentation on a particular topic, you would naturally have to do some research. You would have to learn more about that particular topic to be able to present it with ease and clarity. The last thing you'd want is for audience members to be left scratching their heads, confused and without any understanding of what you're trying to convey, correct? So — pretend you're the presentation. Pretend you're the topic of discussion. What you present is what the world will come to understand as your truth or the truth about you.

A big part of my journey has been learning about being authentic. I'm a big believer that whatever is going on inside you — that's what you shine to the world. Why do you think it becomes very easy for someone to pick up the bad day you're having despite the smile you try to keep on your face? Wouldn't it possibly be better to chat with someone about the bad day versus trying to hide it and therefore compromise authenticity? This isn't to say you're not authentic if you don't. We are all human. We are all prone to the mistakes that humans make. We are not perfect and none of us will ever be. But that is - by far - not an excuse to give up. I think about the mistakes I make daily. I'm very tough on myself. I feel like I should know better at times. I feel like a failure at times. I *feel.* That's a good thing. I learned to have emotion. I learned to be more compassionate. I learned to be more forgiving and understanding. And, I've learned that for as much as I've learned — I have a ton of learning left to do.

My spiritual journey is far from over. For God's sake, I'm not even 40 yet. I don't know when it will end. I've asked my friend Adam for insight regarding this and he couldn't provide a concrete answer. He said it will last for as long as I would like, or for as long as God would like. If my intuition is serving me well, plan on more books! I'm not sure it will ever be over. And there's a reason for that.

Somewhere along the line — within the past year — I've started to come to a realization about where exactly I fit into the world. I have my strengths and I have my weaknesses. Somewhere in the middle of all these pros and cons is a person who genuinely wants to make a difference. I feel compelled to do so. I feel obligated to do so. Most of all, I want to do so. In this realization, I've come to a conclusion. Maybe it's even more than just a conclusion. Maybe it's a Truth I've learned about the Universe. And, I think it's a very important Truth. We are all part of the collective. We are all connected. We are all links in a chain. We all have a part to play. We are all important. We all have duty and obligation. We are all entitled to life. We are all entitled to happiness. We are all movers and shakers. We are built to love, we are meant to console. We are destined to dream and we are obligated to be realistic. We are meant to accomplish and we are driven to achieve. With that said — we can directly affect how our lives — and those of others — play out. How so? Because we are all part of the collective!

Remember as a kid when you would set up dominos in a winding pattern and watch it all collapse when just one domino was knocked into another? Remember that chain-reaction caused when your finger flicked that lead domino? Think of that on a larger scale. Think of yourself as the head domino. Think of your actions and the ripple effect they have in this world. Great or small — your actions cause reactions. Those reactions can be good. Those reactions can also have detrimental effects. You are in control. You send out a vibration into the universe daily. You are part of the collective.

While being very pensive with this concept, I began to get a message. The Universe was trying to tell me something. It was an A-ha moment. And, I needed to listen. It was telling me to wake up daily and do my part. Be authentic. So what's the greater risk if I go against this? Well, aside from being a hypocrite, I would be part of the downfall of society. I would part of the problem. I certainly wouldn't be part of the solution. I used to take the position that as long as people weren't hurting anyone else in this world, they could do whatever they wanted — even hurt themselves by their actions. Again, so long as no one else is hurt in the process. Sounds fair, right? I've scrapped that mentality. It's crap. If you're not pulling your weight in this world — you are depriving the world. You have so much ability, ambition and great intention. By denying that, you're not doing your part. The collective is suffering. It's as simple as that. Doesn't the world deserve you? Don't you deserve to impress the world?

One night while at karaoke, a friend said "great job," on a song I sang. My once self-deprecatory self shrugged it off as just ok. He looked at me and said "stop." He went to tell me there are enough people in this world that will bring me down and I didn't need to contribute to that bunch. How powerful and uplifting is that? And, he's right! If you don't believe in yourself, who will? And, why should anyone believe in you if you don't believe in yourself?

As I explained in the beginning of this book, you gain friends and lose some while on a spiritual journey. At first, I was saddened by it. I truly love my friends and the imprint they leave in the world. But, it's the one they leave on you that really matters. If they're not good for you, then they're not good for you. Plain and simple! Of course it's heartbreaking and sad to say goodbye. Friends build-up one another! They don't cut you down. Friends are proud of your successes, not envious. Friends care unconditionally; not care under certain conditions. If they don't serve you a purpose any longer, or connect with you on the level they once did, maybe it's time to reevaluate. Just be careful! Make sure you've talked it out completely. Maybe even a couple times at that! If that friendship is mean to dissolve, it will. If it's meant to remain in-tact, it will. But you must always surround yourself with the best who want the best for you.

One day while driving to work there was a gorgeous sunrise coming up. I pulled the car over and snapped a photo. I then posted the photo and a little blurb to social media. It said something along the lines of

**"You can look at it as the first sign of another ordinary day. Or, you can see it as a sign to do something out of the ordinary today."**

The next time you're in your kitchen — the heart-of- the - house — sit at the table with the light on. Look at all the places that light touches. It's everywhere. Think of that light as you. When your light is shining bright, look at all the corners, nooks and crannies you have the ability to fill. Now, light a candle and turn the light off. Notice when the light is diminished and just a tiny flame must illuminate the room, a lot of darkness prevails. That darkness now takes over the places where the brighter light once shined. Which light would you rather shine. Do you want people to see your light or be focused on your darkness. That amount of light you shine is up to you. Just remember — it's the exact amount that others will see.

TV reporters get inundated with press releases all the time asking for coverage of a particular event, product launch and so on. At the bottom of a well-written press release is a component called a boiler plate. A boiler plate essentially sums up what a company or brand is all about. It addresses what makes one company stand out from the rest and why the products it carries are important to the world. Boiler plates rarely change much. It's a mantra of sorts for a company to stick to and follow rigorously. Write one for yourself. What do you want to be known as? How do you want the world to view you? Try it. I've included an example below using myself.

**ABOUT MIKE DORIA**
*Mike Doria is a creative, intuitive, uplifting individual working his way through the world in the manner God intended. Using careful judgment, he is a compassionate person who truly wants to make a difference in unique ways. Mike is a believer in mankind, a dreamer and realist. Mike's "to-do" list in life includes: recording an album, writing a screenplay, doing more charity work, skydiving, more travel and learning piano. Mike is thankful for his family, friends, well-being and ability — none of which he takes for granted. Most of all, Mike is appreciative of the blessings from above he's been granted.*

Write one that suits you. In it, include some dreams and goals. Keep it positive and stay proactive. At the end of the day, revisit it. If you're not quite where you want to be, keep trying. If you've fallen away from some of the ideologies — find them again. Remember, you don't fail in life until you quit or give-up. And, if you have given up — there's no rule against a new beginning or starting again. A friend posted on social media one day asking the question whether life came with a reset button. I was intrigued by this idea. I used it as an opportunity to post to my blog. Here's the post titled "Ready, Reset, Go!"

***Every once in a great while — somewhere between the nonsensical update that improves nothing and the***

*inevitable post that's marred by those five damning words "You know who you are," Facebook provides a chance to have an epiphanic moment. This may or may not be one of them — depending on individual levels of intelligence, social superficiality and ability to be open. Anyway, in the news feed the other day I noticed that a very dear friend posted a very plain (but apparently very eye-catching) update asking "Does life have a reset button?" Due to Facebook's uncanny way of getting people to make mountains out of molehills, I stopped for a second — but then proceeded to investigate. Turns out it wasn't a molehill. It was an inroad.*
*As a responsible social media slut I won't name names or provide much detail on the "Why?" behind the post. While the situation was and still is serious — it was also a strategic moment to reach out and cheer someone up.*
*It was a good chance to do what friends do — support outwardly and ridicule quietly. TOTALLY kidding with the ridicule (it was my only moment to attempt humor in this post). Anyway, it got me thinking about life's "Reset" button and whether it exists. It does. We just don't press it enough. Some never press it at all in their journey.*
*In the world of business we have data upon analytics to tell us whether to proceed with a certain model, revamp it or start from scratch. Yet in life, so many of us (including me at times) don't stop to look over data, evaluate and proceed with a "best practices" approach. Therefore, the reset button never gets pushed.*
*Sure, it's difficult to turn around and begin again. You have pride, ego and a whole bunch of other forces playing into that equation. But, find me anyone who is great or an inspiration in this world who hasn't "Reset" and started over. There's a phrase I like that suggests you never fail until you give up. It's genius and so true. So what if it takes a couple of times to learn a lesson or change behaviors or start a business or do whatever. Nowhere in the rule book does it say success must be achieved on the first pass. Plus, if that happened, think*

*of all the other bits and pieces of formidable information with which we'd never cross paths. It's time to replace the bulb in the reset button — get it glowing again to remind us that it's there for using. We can't think of the reset button as a setback. In fact, the sooner we press it sometimes — the sooner we meet our goals and successes. I'm going to start being a little more business minded in my personal life and learn to be more proactive with that often overlooked or dismissed data and analytics. I look forward to pressing the reset button — many times. After all — isn't success for anything the result of doing things repeatedly until getting it right! One final note -- The friend I referred to at the beginning of this post kept his chin up and is doing better. I'm very certain there will come a time in the future where I'll be able to tell you that he is doing amazingly great. For now — Ready, RESET – go!*

The stakes are too high today to sit back and do nothing. The competition in this world is fierce and fearless. However, there is seat at the table for anyone who wants to join. One of my favorite quotes is that from hotel mogul Steve Wynn. "Bigger isn't better. Better is better." Create a can do attitude. Work hard. Enjoy life and find balance. The world can't afford to lose you. Let's see the **new guy** or gal. You can't afford to lose you!

Be good. Be safe. Be giving. God Bless!

# ACKNOWLEDGEMENTS

While there are many people in my life to thank for being part of the reason, behind this book – I'd like to point out some of the most important.

As a child, I met Adam Christ in the fourth grade. Now approaching 40 years old in just a couple years, we still talk all the time. He's never let me off the hook when I was being a jerk and never let me go with accolades on my accomplishments. Our spiritual journeys couldn't be more different, yet more alike at the same time.

In high school, I had English teachers who only saw the best in what I had to offer the writing world. Mrs. Przybycien, Mrs. Gamble and Mrs. Hinman – thank you all for the "A" papers and your encouragement.

While in college, my journalism professor Virginia Bacheler, was often aggravated by my non-stop questions with all things journalism. After graduation, she called me back several times to speak to her classes. Thank you for being the greatest inspiration and believer one could ask for. I'm grateful daily for your insight and all you've taught me. I hope I've made you proud.

Shaliz Koleini was my fellow reporter on the morning team at Fox 5 News. She and her husband, Robert Afshar gave me the most valuable two cents I needed to hear. "Do what you're passionate about in life." From that point on, I hit the ground running. You two are 100 percent amazing!

The world would not be a very nice place with the incredible Kristen Miranda. I look up to you so much and can't thank you for all your love, support and words of wisdom. Even in my darkest hours, you've been there with open arms. I'm forever grateful for our friendship.

To my father, brother and sister: I know that what I do or am doing doesn't often make sense, but know that it is all part of my destiny. My greatest accomplishment in life was learning to spread my wings and fly wherever. But, your never ending support along the way has been the best air on which to glide. I love you.

To my nephew Michael Doria. Man, I can't wait to see the kind of amazing, determined adult I know you'll grow into. You have so much power you've yet to realize. From the minute I learned you'd be named after me, I was elated. When I first held you, it was magical. I'm proud to be your uncle.

# ABOUT THE AUTHOR

Michael Ferdinand Joseph Doria is an American author, writer and journeyman through life. He was born February 27th, 1976 in Rochester, NY to Ferdinand and Nancy Doria. He is the middle-child with an older sister Gina Doria Foster and younger brother Anthony Doria. Michael graduated from Brockport State University in 1998 with a Bachelors Degree in Broadcast Journalism. He spent 11 years as a TV News Reporter before changing career fields to Public Relations & Marketing. Doria's fascination with writing and interacting with people has also included two music albums. He has plans to write a children's book series, more books on spirituality and self-help and a screenplay. Doria's blog titled "Blah, Blah Blog" and audio component titled "Mike Check" can be found at www.mikedoria.com

Made in the USA
Charleston, SC
30 December 2013